Praise for
Awakening from the Daydream

"A wonderful book—pithy, relevant, and fun to read."
—Sharon Salzberg, author of *Lovingkindness*

"The Buddhist wheel of life reveals a tragic human irony—
that we humans author the very distress we are seeking
to avoid. As a heart-son of Chögyam Trungpa Rinpoche,
David is uniquely equipped to help us explore and
unravel this profound truth—his lively wisdom and sharp
humor is exactly what we need in these difficult times."
—Michael Carroll, author of *Awake at Work*

"Imagine yourself deeply asleep in a dormitory filled with
everyone in the whole world. From way down inside your
darkness, you hear a voice sweetly calling your name...
'Hey! My friend, time to get up. Time to get up. Come out
and play!' You slowly open your tired eyes a little and see
the smiling face of your friend calling to you. That is this
book, calling out to wake us from our dreamy slumber."
—Krishna Das, kirtan vocalist

"David Nichtern is one of the most effortless and effective teachers I have ever met. He's funny and smart, which I love, but even better he uses his humor and intelligence to transmit a deeper message that can truly change your life. Get into it!"
—Pete Holmes, comedian and host of *You Made It Weird*

"As a long-time Buddhist practitioner, there are a few people I have turned to over and over to help me make sense of the Dharma, and David Nichtern is one of them. His insights comfort and shock in equal measure, and this book is no exception. If you are looking for an introduction to the Buddhist path that is both gentle and fierce, this is the book for you. Using the iconic Wheel of Life as the gateway, it goes beyond the academic to offer real-life insights into how to transform your suffering into wisdom and joy. I'm so happy this book exists. PS, he is incredibly funny."
—Susan Piver, author of *Start Here Now* and founder of the Open Heart Project

Awakening from the Daydream

Awakening from the Daydream

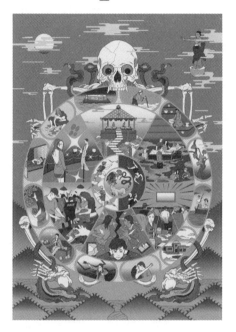

REIMAGINING THE BUDDHA'S WHEEL OF LIFE

David Nichtern

WITH AN ESSAY BY CHÖGYAM TRUNGPA

Wisdom

Wisdom Publications
199 Elm Street
Somerville, MA 02144 USA
wisdomexperience.org

Library of Congress Cataloging-in-Publication Data
Names: Nichtern, David, author.
Title: Awakening from the daydream : reimagining the Buddha's wheel of life / David Nichtern.
Description: Somerville, MA : Wisdom Publications, [2016]
Identifiers: LCCN 2016010336| ISBN 9781614290056 (pbk. : alk. paper) | ISBN 9781614290063 (ebook) | ISBN 1614290059
Subjects: LCSH: Buddhist eschatology. | Karma.
Classification: LCC BQ4506 .N53 2016 | DDC 294.3/422--dc23
LC record available at https://lccn.loc.gov/2016010336

ISBN 978-1-61429-005-6   ebook ISBN 978-1-61429-006-3

24 23 22   6 5 4

Wheel of Life illustration by Andrew Archer, UNA: www.usenewart.com. Cover design by Gopa&Ted2, Inc. Interior design by Jordan Wannemacher. Set in Arnhem Pro 9.8 pt. /15 pt.

Please visit fscus.org.

Contents

Introduction

THE WHEEL OF LIFE is a Buddhist allegorical painting dating back to ancient India. The painting describes how our sense of self and our life in this world take shape, portraying how we think, how we act, how we feel, and how we manifest our own personal reality. The Wheel of Life also illustrates how karma works in our lives—how we get trapped in confusing, painful, and repetitive patterns, and how we can liberate ourselves from those patterns.

The essence of the Wheel allegory is that our lives are heavily influenced by the internal dramas that we project onto them. We ourselves create a "daydream" world in which we live most of the time. Just as we experience dreams as if they were reality while dreaming, we experience the daydream of our lives to be real and react to it accordingly: "That person doesn't like me, so I feel depressed," or "I'm in love and now everything is going to be perfect." We are rarely, if ever, aware of how much our own mental habits fabricate and distort our experience of life. We do not see the situation clearly. It's as if we wear special glasses made of all of our thoughts, feelings, impulses, and so on, that color and distort how we see our lives. The good news is that, given that these glasses are of our own making, we can remove them and awaken from our daydream world.

MY EXPERIENCE WITH THE WHEEL

I first started studying Buddhism in 1970 when I met Chögyam Trungpa Rinpoche. At the time, I was attending the Berklee College of Music in Boston and was also studying yoga at the East/West Yoga Studio on Marlborough Street. I met Trungpa Rinpoche fairly soon after his arrival in the United States when he came to our yoga studio to lead a seminar called "Work, Sex, and Money."

It seemed funny to me at the time that a high lama from Tibet would be talking about such things, even more so when he showed up in a business suit and talked about the inseparability of spiritual practice and our everyday lives. In those early days, he travelled around the United States, gave a variety of seminars, mentored people individually, and attracted a diverse group of students.

One of the seminars he gave in those early days was on the Wheel of Life, at the Tail of the Tiger (now Karmê Chöling) Meditation Center in Barnet, Vermont. The seminar was given at the town hall recreation center, which had a basketball hoop in it! It was summertime and we would walk back and forth from the meditation center to town to attend the lectures.

I remember how big an impression the Wheel of Life teachings made on me when I first heard them. I was totally blown away by how precisely and completely the portrait of the six realms exactly described the diverse experiences of my daily dramas. Any mood, memory, or expectation could be placed into one of the six settings: blissing out with the warmth and fragrance of summer was to enter the god realm; feeling claustrophobic and burned out by the intensity of the schedule, the practice, and the food was to sojourn in hell; craving the company of one of the lovely young women there or a bittersweet chocolate bar was to fall into the hungry ghost realm right on the spot!

I remember walking down the road to the retreat center and thinking about how intimidating the material was. It was as if Rinpoche were lecturing directly to me. He seemed to know all of my neurotic patterns and knew how to resolve them. He was killing me softly with my own song! I remember thinking that I had nowhere to hide. In the end I felt compelled to renounce it all and become a monk. Of course, I managed to regroup and continue to inhabit the six realms for the next forty years or so, but at that time I could not imagine going on with it. There really seemed to be no point at all in continuing to hang out in these familiar, repetitive patterns now that I recognized them for what they were.

Other practitioners in the past and present have had that kind of recognition and decided to instantly cut all ties to these six realms of samsara. There are famous stories about this kind of radical renunciation throughout the history of Buddhism. The most common version is somebody becoming a monk or nun and dedicating his or her entire life to practice and study. They abandon all hope of seeking satisfaction in the six realms in a very literal way.

Obviously, joining a monastery would have been a radical step, but it was well beyond my own spiritual capacity and ambition. Fortunately, there is a path for householders like myself, and there are clearly outlined practices for navigating our lives within the six realms, as we work our way, little by little, toward awakening. The original painting of the Wheel was given to a king rather than to a monk, after all. The lay approach to Buddhist practice allows us to see the imprisoning aspect of the six realms, but to recognize the seed of wisdom and transformational possibilities within them as well. Having sat with and returned to the allegory of the Wheel as the basis of my practice for many years, I decided to incorporate the Wheel into my own teachings.

For the past fifteen years or so I have taught workshops based on the Wheel of Life. Given that the crux of the allegory is that we spend the majority of our time living within the fantasies that we ourselves unconsciously project on the world, I called my workshops "Awakening From the Daydream: The Wheel of Life."

ORIGINS AND MESSAGE OF THE WHEEL

The Wheel of Life uses traditional Buddhist cosmological imagery to convey its allegory. There are six distinct "realms" within the wheel. Each realm represents a particular state of mind that shapes and limits our notions of what is real and what is possible. Our minds and our external situations mirror each other in the process, structuring our basic psychology.

Tradition says that the Buddha directed the creation of the original Wheel painting, which he commissioned as a gift to teach Dharma to an Indian king. When the king who received the painting contemplated it and fully understood its meaning, he attained enlightenment—he brought the suffering caused by unconscious habitual patterns to an end. Since then the Wheel has been painted countless times and has become a standard image displayed at the entryway to Buddhist temples all over Asia. The image has remained popular down through the ages because it makes subtle Buddhist teachings about the working of the mind accessible to the lay masses. The image of the Wheel survives not just because it sustains tradition, but because the message it conveys is powerful and timelessly relevant.

In modern terms we might think of the Wheel as a kind of PowerPoint presentation: it is a concise collection of information-rich points that provide a comprehensive overview of our existential state. Karma, an overarching theme of the Wheel image, means "action" or "work." Karma describes how our world works, how different realities come into being, and how they change. The agent behind the work of karma is the mind, all the habitual thoughts, perspectives, and impulses that drive our behavior and experience. Karma explains how we became who we were in the past, how we become who we are now, and how we become who we will be in the future. The working of karma is a mostly unconscious process: our habits are shaped by past experiences, which in turn shape our present behavior such that we find ourselves facing familiar situations in the present. The repetition of unproductive patterns, the cycle of familiar mental and behavioral landscapes, is called samsara.

Sometimes tropical fish in a tank leave a tiny thin trail of poop behind them as they swim around the tank. Once they have completed one cycle around, all of a sudden the poop is right in front of them. This is how karma works. You can almost imagine the fish saying to herself, "Now where did that come from?" In this metaphor, that fish is us, the fish tank is samsara, and the poop is the result of our habitual behavior.

Uninterrupted by fresh input that would break the chain, these karmic cycles go on and on. This idea is not unfamiliar to modern psychology. The Buddha's essential message was that largely unconscious forces drive our unawakened lives, placing us in unpleasant situations and surroundings over and over again. This is why samsara is depicted as an endlessly turning wheel that only stops rolling when we awaken to the forces that drive it. The allegory of the Wheel reveals potent insight into how we get stuck cycling through psychological and emotional landscapes and tells us how to cultivate positive tendencies that help free us from ingrained karmic patterns.

My goal in this book is to present these ancient teachings in more contemporary language, with imagery more immediately recognizable to modern readers. The illustration of the Wheel used in the book depicts modern people in contemporary settings to convey the psychological tone of each of the six realms. This approach is very much in keeping with how I myself learned about the six realms from my teacher, Chögyam Trungpa Rinpoche.

THE SIX REALMS

Many people these days are exploring being mindful, present, and aware in the moment. But where are we when we are not present in the moment? We are lost in the daydream landscapes we have created in our minds. The Wheel of Life breaks our wandering in samsara down into six distinct realms that mirror our own inner psychological and emotional landscape. There is nothing random about the six realms. We are the co-creators of these environments, based on past and present thoughts and actions—based on our karma.

The six realms depicted in the wheel are

1. The God Realm
2. The Jealous God Realm
3. The Human Realm
4. The Animal Realm
5. The Hungry Ghost Realm
6. The Hell Realm

Traditionally Buddhist cultures have treated the Wheel of Life as representative of a real cosmology, wherein the six realms are actual, objective destinies into which one might be born. In this view the six realms represent six different kinds of environment, physical body, and mental state that we might occupy based on karma from past lives. For example, you may be reborn in the sea as a dolphin if you are born in the animal realm, or you may be reborn as a being with a huge belly and a tiny mouth and neck that lives in a barren graveyard setting where you experience great loneliness and deprivation if you are born in the hungry ghost realm. This way of looking at the Wheel of Life presupposes belief in reincarnation and multiple planes of physical reality. It will likely be difficult for people who are not from traditionally Buddhist cultures to adopt this view.

On the other hand, we can look at the six realms as a creative and fruitful way of describing the circumstances of our day-to-day realities. From this point of view the realms are seen as psychological landscapes that we migrate through over time; the realms are our internal mood, our attitudes, and habitual patterns projected out onto the world, where we mistake them for reality. We may move through a realm over the course of an hour, a day, a month, a year, and so on, depending on how deeply ingrained the particular mental state that drives the realm may be. If we succumb to depressive thoughts and feel that the world is against us, we may slide into a hell realm. Similarly, if we are dominated by emotions like jealousy and pride, our friends may turn into enemies as we move into the hypercompetitive realm of the jealous gods.

Although personally I have no problem relating to the exoteric or literal understanding of the realms, I would like to focus, in this book, on the realms as an allegory for the power of unchecked mental habits to distort our experience of the world, and will treat them in this way throughout this book. You needn't believe in reincarnation or higher or lower planes of existence to use the teachings presented here. The principal work we will undertake in the coming pages will be to develop a greater understanding of how our own psychology and emotions affect our experiences in life, and using that understanding to change our thoughts and actions so that we have a happier and more expansive life. We will be talking about what goes on in our day-to-day lives, how it can sometimes work against us, and how we can make it work for us.

ABOUT KARMA

Karma is an essential theme in the Wheel of Life. Understanding karma is as simple as seeing that what we think, say, and do directly affects our experiences in life. The law of karma describes the precise relationship between actions and their consequences. It is always at play in both the short and long term. Karma, like the law of gravity, exists whether we know it or not. It is just so. It is how things naturally occur.

Whether our actions are virtuous or not is not determined by some superior, external, cosmic authority, but by the results that our actions naturally bring. Selfish behavior tends to bring mental turmoil, such as fear of reprisal or guilt, and physical difficulty, such as being shunned or physically attacked. From the Buddhist point of view, we are each responsible for our own situation, whether we care to admit it or not. We are all active participants in the creation of our own karma. We all have the capacity to determine our future paths. This is a very empowering way of looking at our world. In Buddha's time this view was revolutionary and directly opposed the Indian caste system of the times, which suggested that the fate of individuals was mostly fixed by the particularities of the station they were born into.

The Wheel of Life is essentially a portrait of how karma

works. Studying it can help us to better understand how our actions have impacted our lives and to choose better ways of acting to ensure a happier future. By developing a deeper understanding of karma, we can learn to free ourselves from unconscious and repetitive reliance on outdated and unproductive patterns of thought and behavior.

THE ROLE OF MEDITATION

Meditation and contemplation are powerful tools that can help us to clearly see the daydream-like realms that we project and to awaken from that daydream. Meditation is not a monolithic practice; there are many different types of meditation. In general, *meditation* helps us become more familiar with our intuitive awareness and *contemplation* helps us focus our thought to develop clarity and insight. As we work through the realms in the chapters to come, I will present meditation techniques that will help us to navigate the particular challenges of the mindsets that drive each realm.

The formal practice of sitting meditation allows us to look directly at our minds' activity, to recognize how often the power of our thoughts and emotions carry us away from reality. Periodically, in our meditation, and sometimes in daily life, we actually awaken from our daydream mind, and experience a clear moment of being awake and present, free from the filter of thoughts and preconceptions. Experiencing the moment in this way is the mindfulness that so many people write about these days: a simple moment of awareness unfettered by memories of the past and projections about the future. Recognizing this moment—recognizing and expanding the experience—was and still is the essence of the Buddha's teachings.

The discovery of this kind of direct awareness is sometimes described as finding a treasure hidden in plain sight or a precious jewel in a garbage dump. The most magical and powerful experience imaginable can be discovered right here in the middle of the mess and turmoil we call our everyday lives.

ONE

A Brief Overview
of the Wheel

BEFORE WE DIVE into a detailed exploration of the six realms, let's take a short tour of the whole Wheel to get oriented.

IMPERMANENCE: THE "GRIM REAPER"— HE'S GOT THE WHOLE WORLD IN HIS HANDS

As you can see, in our updated representation, the "Grim Reaper" (here depicted as a skeleton) is holding the entire wheel in his hands. In the traditional diagram of the wheel, a wrathful, demonic figure who represents death and impermanence holds the wheel in his mouth. The Grim Reaper holding the wheel indicates that each ring of the wheel, in fact, every aspect of our lives, is governed by impermanence.

The fact that impermanence and change govern our lives might seem obvious. It is less obvious that much of the confusion and anxiety we experience in our everyday lives comes from resisting change. Resistance to change creates suffering.

Folk wisdom tells us that death of a loved one, moving away from home, and divorce are the three major traumas most commonly faced in life. We can fill out this picture with further details, like aging, sickness, injury, job loss, conflict, war, heartbreak, and financial collapse. We could all add in our own categories here, as we all surely have our own unique little set of annoyances that occur from day to day. All of these varieties of suffering revolve around being confronted with impermanence and change.

When we lose something we want, we suffer. When we gain something we don't want, we suffer. When we vacillate between wanting to get something and wanting to get rid of something, we suffer. Underneath all of this is a vague feeling of uncertainty about the whole situation, which is another kind of suffering—the suffering of existential stress or anxiety. The relationship between impermanence and suffering is one of the broadest aspects of the Wheel and arguably of Buddhism altogether. When His Holiness the Sixteenth Karmapa, one of the truly great Buddhist masters of the twentieth century, was asked what an enlightened person experienced, he simply answered, "Impermanence."

THE HUB OF THE WHEEL: PASSION, AGGRESSION, AND IGNORANCE

The inner portions of the wheel are made up of concentric rings that contain various images representing different aspects of these teachings. In traditional diagrams of the wheel, the centermost ring—the hub—contains the image of three animals: a rooster, a snake, and a pig. Each animal holds the next one's tail in its mouth to form a circle.

The rooster, snake, and pig represent passion, aggression, and ignorance. The rooster represents passion, grasping, or attachment, the snake represents aggression or aversion, and the pig represents ignorance or indifference. These three animal metaphors illustrate the ways we categorize and respond to others and our environment at the most basic level. These responses are called the three "root obscurations" or *mulakleshas* in traditional Buddhism, because they obscure our natural awareness and clarity about who we are, who others are, and what we are doing. The obscurations are dynamic rather than static feelings. Passion (grasping) is the desire to include, aggression (aggressing) is the desire to exclude, and ignorance (ignoring) happens when we don't particularly notice or care one way or the other.

It is actually possible to categorize every thought we have, every attitude, as one or a combination of two or more of these three core responses. For example, if you fall in love with somebody, you might feel that you want to include them in every activity of your life (grasping), yet you might want to get rid of attitudes or habits that they have that annoy you (aggressing), and don't really want to see other flaws and faults that might turn into big problems later on (ignoring).

In general our responses to what are essentially momentary experiences tend to solidify over time. For example, a friend at the office might criticize some aspect of my work. Taking offense at this, I begin to see that person as a competitor, or even my enemy. Once I feel that someone is an enemy, I actively try to avoid or discredit him or her. When others maliciously gossip about them, I relish it and add a few lines of my own to the chatter. In this way my basic response solidifies and begins to affect how I think and act.

Our compulsion to act on and solidify basic responses creates a mental residue called karma. It is the part of our interaction with the world that is left over and colors our future experience. Karma is created by lingering desire, lingering aggression, and ignored or repressed experiences that drift into the background of our consciousness, only to return to the foreground when causes and conditions are ripe. It is difficult to see other people and situations clearly with that kind of residue lingering in our mind. Our karmic residue also prevents us from feeling unbiased affection, interest, or appreciation. These three ingrained habits of grasping, aggressing, and ignoring work to shut down our hearts and minds.

On the other hand, each of the three obscurations has a flip side that is relatively more wise and discerning. According to the Buddhist teachings, we can distill enlightened aspects from these obscurations and transform our confusion into wisdom. The transformation of passion is what draws us closer to others, the transformation of aggression is what allows us to cut away that which is not healthy, and the transformation of ignorance is what allows us to be accommodating and spacious.

POSITIVE AND NEGATIVE ACTIONS

The next ring off center in the wheel portrays positive and negative actions. In the traditional diagram a line of people being led toward the upper part of the wheel by a monk symbolizes positive actions and a line of people being bound and dragged toward the lower part of the wheel by a demon symbolizes negative actions. In this updated version of the wheel, positive and negative actions are symbolized by a duo of boy scouts climbing toward the upper part of the wheel and a man being roped and dragged to the lower part of the wheel, respectively.

Very simply, the ten positive actions are based on acting with awareness, sympathy, clarity, and compassion. These actions create a relatively positive result in the form of benefit to oneself and others. The ten negative actions, generated by grasping, aggressing, and ignoring, create a relatively negative result in the form of causing harm to ourselves and others. Most of what it takes to understand the impact of our actions is common sense.

THE SIX REALMS

The next ring outward in the wheel is divided into six sections, like a pie. Each section depicts life in one of the six realms. The realms are portraits of six different styles of interacting with the world; they are six different settings in which we hang out for minutes, hours, days, weeks, months, maybe even years. On the one hand the realms really take shape in our minds as a set of moods, attitudes, and emotional landscapes. On the other hand they are reflected in our external environment as dwellings, contexts, clothing, transportation, companions, neighborhoods, etc. Once we are in a realm, that particular quality of life begins to feel very familiar, very normal.

So, again—the six realms are

1. The God Realm
2. The Jealous God Realm
3. The Human Realm
4. The Animal Realm
5. The Hungry Ghost Realm
6. The Hell Realm

In general the realms are characterized by our relationship to pleasure and pain. When we are able to experience an extremely pleasurable quality of life for stable, sustained periods of time, this is known as the god realm, and in some sense it is considered the pinnacle of life within samsara. The jealous gods experience a less stable yet still pleasurable environment so there is lots of insecurity, competition, and envy. The humans have passion, longing, and curiosity and fluctuate between pleasure and pain. The animals stubbornly try to recreate familiar patterns of pleasurable circumstances while avoiding suffering. The hungry ghosts seek pleasurable circumstances but experience mostly craving and dissatisfaction. Finally, the hell realm beings experience almost continuous stress, anxiety, aggression, and depression.

THE CHAIN OF CAUSE AND EFFECT

The outermost ring of the wheel is called in Sanskrit the *nidanas*, the chain of interdependent origination, or dependent arising. This ring describes how we move from ignorance to birth, old age, sickness, and death, over and over again. It is yet another way of describing how karma develops through particular causes creating particular effects, and how each of those effects becomes a cause of the next link in the cycle.

THE BUDDHA IN EACH REALM

In the original Wheel, there is a Buddha teaching the inhabitants of each realm, speaking a language they can understand based on the quality of their experience. The Buddhas represent the possibility for us to develop insight, wisdom, and compassion, regardless of our circumstances.

In the traditional iconography, each realm has a Buddha in a different guise, teaching the beings of that realm how to transform their circumstances. The Buddha represents the qualities of enlightenment, expressed in a way that will be accessible to the beings within that particular mindset. For example, the Buddha in the jealous god realm is holding a sword of wisdom. Even when we are caught up in competitiveness and aggression, we might still be able to access a feeling of sharpness and power in terms of dealing with people and situations, enabling us to sometimes move beyond purely selfish motivation, and leading us toward developing qualities that can bring out the best in ourselves and others.

The Buddha in the hungry ghost realm is holding sustenance in a vial and is presenting the virtue of generosity. When we are in the hungry ghost realm we are completely stuck in a cycle based on our own sense of impoverishment and low self-esteem, so the ideas of having even moderate satisfaction and of being generous to others can be liberating for us.

In the human realm, as mentioned, there is enough openness to actually allow us to hear new ideas, develop insight, and change old patterns. The Buddha in the human realm is sometimes depicted as holding a begging bowl, representing the wandering mendicant who takes the teachings to heart and develops renunciation from the purely materialistic lifestyle, in order to develop greater spiritual realization.

There is also usually a Buddha standing outside of the wheel, representing transcending the six realms altogether. Such people are said to be free from imprisonment in the six realms—free of karma—and only appear in the six realms in order to teach and liberate the beings within the realms out of compassion. Sometimes we are fortunate enough to meet people who remind us of this kind of possibility.

The role of the Buddhas in the Wheel is to point to the possibility of transforming our experience within each realm, which we revisit throughout the book. We can either see our karma and our life in the realms as imprisonment or we can see them as the opportunity for liberation: it is completely up to us.

THE CYCLE OF CONFUSION AND SUFFERING AND THE WAY OUT

The Wheel portrays the different ways we get trapped in repetitive patterns and imprison ourselves emotionally, intellectually, and in relation to our external life circumstances. In addition to describing the form of our imprisonment, the Wheel also points to a pathway out, to freedom, liberation, true peace, and real happiness.

The root cause of our experience in the realms is none other than our own state of mind, our own consciousness. For example, we can be in luxurious circumstances and still be in a hellish state of mind. Perhaps we can think of someone who has tremendously fortunate circumstances in his or her life who is nonetheless unhappy, dissatisfied, maybe even depressed or suicidal. On the other hand we might know someone who has had tremendously challenging circumstances, all kinds of obstacles, financial hardships, and yet is fundamentally peaceful, wise, and compassionate. By these examples we can see clearly that our environment influences our consciousness, but it also seems to have its own independent basis. Working with our mind is possible in any situation, and that is the very powerful redemptive message of the Wheel teachings. The notion of transforming confusion into wisdom, obstacles into opportunities, and changing our world in the process is the central message here.

Each realm holds a key to understanding the "issues" of that particular setting and a way to move beyond the obstacles and obscurations that confine us there.

TWO

Daydreaming the Six Realms

SIX TYPES OF DAYDREAM

While we are experiencing the six realms, they feel powerfully and completely real. We take our established pattern of existence to be the norm and don't often imagine transforming our situation beyond that norm.

Our experience of the realms is strongly supported by our internal dialogue. We are always telling ourselves a story. When we experience the jealous god realm, our mind is occupied with comparison, evaluation, and competitive logic. When we experience the hell realm, we constantly repeat a litany of hardships, complaints, and regrets. When we experience the human realm, we are always strategizing our lives, trying to figure out how to solve our relationship dramas or get the right job or career path.

Seeing this kind of activity in our minds clearly is the key to understanding how the realms take shape and thrive. It is also powerful to see how our sense of environment is at least partially created as a reflection of our minds. As the situation around us solidifies and takes shape, it will undoubtedly influence the course of our thoughts and emotions. We then continue to shape the external situation based on our own perception and projections. Our minds influence the environment, and the environment influences our minds. Through this loop the realms develop tremendous power. Our internal landscape and the external situation are reinforcing each other and creating a particular mood and setting that define the experience of the six realms.

In a mostly unconscious way, we carry the tone of each realm within us as a kind of baseline or ground hum of existence. The quality of each realm is not completely accurate; our experience is filtered by our habits and projections, and from there the situation becomes a self-fulfilling prophecy. Each realm actually contours our thoughts, feelings, and perceptions, which in turn shape our expectations and new experiences as they arise.

This contouring of mood and tone is like the flavor of a particular dream we might have, in which there is an underlying tone of anxiety, pain, craving, envy, or even happiness or bliss. We might wake up with a particular feeling that can take some time to shake off. That tone can, at times, be more informative than the content of the dream itself. It is relatively easy to assess this tone from our dreams. It is harder and subtler to notice the quality and texture of our waking life and to be aware of the fact that we are, in some sense, still dreaming.

This daydream world that we call reality consists of the shapes and experiences of the six realms. We might feel powerful anxiety or depression related to circumstances that do not seem to warrant that response (hell realm), or we might be obsessed with pleasurable circumstances—either stabilizing them (god realm) or craving them (hungry ghost). The six realms are settings for our mind, and we have forgotten that we have applied those filters. Practicing meditation can help us remove these filters and experience our reality more clearly.

PLEASURE AND PAIN AND EVERYTHING IN BETWEEN

The two powerful poles of experience that define our journey through the realms are pleasure (what we seek) and pain (what we seek to avoid). Pleasure can range in intensity from the mildest feeling of writing a check with money in the bank, to having a great dinner, to meeting the love of your life, to a feeling of bliss and peace that goes beyond anything we have experienced before. Pain also comes as a spectrum of experience, ranging from a splinter in our finger, to a broken heart, to a twenty-four-hour flu, to feeling our life or the life of a loved one slipping away. All of these experiences are inescapable parts of our ordinary human lives. What all the pleasurable experiences have in common is that we welcome them and find them desirable. In the case of the range of painful experiences, what they have in common is that we would like to avoid them.

When we experience the highest realms—the realms of the gods and the jealous gods—seeking and sustaining pleasurable circumstances is our highest priority. Of course that approach goes hand-in-hand with avoiding painful circumstances, even if they might signify the opportunity to learn something new or develop insight and empathy. When we experience the three lower realms—the realms of the animal, hungry ghost, and hell beings—the desire to avoid pain is stronger. Our attempts to achieve and stabilize pleasurable circumstances become progressively less effective as we go lower in the realms, so that in the hell realm we cannot imagine any situation in which we can experience pleasure, ease, or even a glimpse of satisfaction.

The realms, however, are evolved out of our initial and simple assessment of every experience as either pleasurable or painful. As we experience each of the realms, we create scenarios built around our relationship to our experiences. In the following chapters we will have an in-depth look at each realm in regard to the quality, tone, and texture of these scenarios. The exact same situation can be framed completely differently based on our attitude and our previous experience.

Our self-portrait as it unfolds within the realms can be penetrating and intense. We are talking about how our whole lives take shape and evolve, from cradle to grave. This is literally a life and death situation, so exploring the realms is a serious matter. However, in the spirit of just getting familiar with the psychology of the realms, let's start by taking a look at what the relatively harmless experience of eating a bowl of chocolate ice cream might feel like in each of the realms.

Sometimes there is no obstacle whatsoever to enjoyment. We seem to be able to get whatever we want whenever we want it. Certainly we've all had those moments where we felt like we had won the lottery. For some, unfettered enjoyment may manifest in their environment: ring a silver bell and ice cream miraculously appears from the kitchen, served on fine china with silver spoons and elegantly embroidered napkins. For others, even the cheapest ice cream served in a Styrofoam bowl will completely meet and exceed their desires. This is the god realm—enjoyment so pure that we feel as if we are in heaven.

Then there are those times when we can really only enjoy something after we have made sure that it's actually worthy of our enjoyment. We know what's good in life because we've read up on it, kept up with what's desirable, and only settle for the best. There are those who go out of their way to find the very best ice cream and insist on eating only a particular, exotic type of Brazilian chocolate with a certain percentage of dark unprocessed cacao and organic cow's milk from Vermont. Or consider the simpler summertime example that we've all surely had: Mom buys ice cream for each child, but somehow, despite the fact that the ice cream is the same, mine just seems like it doesn't taste as good when I see that my brother has a bigger serving. The whole experience is tainted by this desire to have the best, to be on top, to be the winner. This is the jealous god realm—enjoyment threatened by neverending competition.

Sometimes our ability to truly enjoy things is counterbalanced by the cold, hard facts of life. Of course everybody wants the best in life, but we have to be practical. I may want the best kind of ice cream available, but considering my waistline, cholesterol, and so on, I have second thoughts. Maybe I should go with a yogurt or tofu option instead. Or maybe I just wait until no one is watching and eat the good stuff secretly. Embarrassment, guilt, and all kinds of second thoughts come quickly on the heels of most forms of pleasure. This is the human realm—pleasure and pain come in equal measure and take turns controlling our state of mind.

Then there are the times when our indulgence in pleasures is little more than instinctual. We fall into familiar patterns that tend toward the pleasure of comfort in the face of the dull pain of everyday life. Surely we've all had that late Friday night after a long, hard week, when we just want to put our feet up and have some ice cream while we watch our favorite program on TV. Before we know it, eating one spoonful after another without paying much attention, we've finished off half the carton! Many of us have mindless comfort-eating habits or comfort-television-watching habits. This is the animal realm—working to keep the pain of a dull existence at bay with the pleasure of mindless comfort.

Sometimes the object of our desire seems to always be just out of reach. The more we try to get what we want, the further away it seems, and the frustration of not being able to satisfy ourselves eats away at us. Imagine waking up late at night with a craving for chocolate ice cream. You know you have a carton in the freezer, but it turns out that someone has already eaten the last of it. The fact that there is none makes you want the ice cream even more. You head out to pick some up from the local 24-hour grocer, only to find that the store is closed on this particular day. We've all had this type of experience, whether it's a lovelorn heart or failing to make the cut after three rounds of tryouts. This is the hungry ghost realm—unquenchable desire for what is always just beyond our reach.

There are also those times when life seems so bleak that the possibility of ever enjoying anything ever again seems exceedingly remote. After the loss of a loved one or a particularly intense breakup, we may plunge into a severe depression. Even if a friend asked us out to ice cream in an attempt to raise our spirits, it would be unlikely that we would enjoy even a spoonful of it. Under the black cloud of depression, the very idea of enjoyment seems foreign and unreal. This is the hell realm—we are so far removed from enjoyment and pleasure that we feel like we are in hell.

OUR PRECIOUS HUMAN LIVES

The human realm is considered to be unique among the six, because the experience of vacillating between pleasure and pain leaves us uncertain about the basis of our existence.

We fluctuate between having and not having, between knowing and not knowing, between hope and fear. Our minds are full of discursive thoughts and story lines, little movies about our lives that play over and over again. There is a strong sense of being the narrator, telling the stories of our life continuously with slight modifications and variations each time. Sometimes we appear to be winning, sometimes losing, and sometimes it's hard to tell.

The ongoing fluctuation between hope and fear can leave us feeling vulnerable and insecure but can also cause us to be curious, adventurous, and therefore possibly open to seeking insight and transformation. The human realm contains the potential for passionate inquiry, for reaching out beyond our particular comfort zone to explore our world. It is the only realm in which we allow the question of "who am I?" to ripen.

Philosophy, psychology, inquiry, debate, etc., are prominent interests for those experiencing the human realm. It is the least solid and most uncertain of all the realms, but ironically it is here that we have the opportunity to know ourselves more fully and to understand and change our patterns of behavior. The human realm is traditionally considered the most opportune of all the realms in which to attain realization or enlightenment, precisely because it fosters the qualities of inquiry and exploration. It is here that we have the chance to learn about our situation more completely, meet teachers, study, practice, and begin to wake up from the daydream of the six realms. This is why human life is considered auspicious, rare, and precious from the perspective of traditional Buddhism, and why a human realm mindset is so desirable.

EVERYDAY LIFE AND THE SIX REALMS

Studying the six realms can help us understand our everyday lives. Samsara is cyclical in nature: we engage in the same actions again and again and experience their results again and again. Samsara is driven by habitual behavior. For example, you might find yourself periodically having the same argument with someone close to you. The words and emotions used in the argument may be so familiar that it feels like you are playing back a recording of an earlier event.

The feeling that we are blindly repeating patterns of thought, emotion, and behavior is the hallmark of samsaric existence. Our daydream world, with the familiar storylines we weave into it, actually keeps us one step removed from vividly experiencing the moment as it occurs. Tuning in to the Wheel teachings helps us to begin to see the dreamlike qualities of life—to see the dreamlike realms of experience that we cycle through and to awaken from our daydream.

MEDITATION PRACTICE AND THE SIX REALMS

As we develop clarity about our experience of the six realms and come to understand that being trapped in them is inherently painful, we naturally tend to seek relief from these ultimately claustrophobic patterns. Meditation is very helpful in this regard. Meditation allows us to create a space in which we can recognize our daydreams as they occur and avoid being trapped in them.

While experiencing any of six realms, some portion of our minds remains open and aware. No matter how deeply we may be immersed in a given realm, this purity of mind remains. Perhaps you have had the experience of being heavily engaged in an argument, competing with your adversary in a heated debate where emotions run high, and recognizing, despite the intense agitation within your mind, that you can see the whole situation from a much broader, less engaged point of view. Most of us have had this type of experience where some part of ourselves seems to be watching from a distance. Meditation is a tool with which we cultivate and strengthen this kind of "abstract watcher," so that we can purposefully shift our perspective in order to have a clearer and more complete picture of our situation.

Typically the habits that we have formed are quite strong, quickly activated by circumstances in our lives, and therefore govern our basic patterns of behavior. However, there is always a tiny gap between stimulus and our reaction to it, even in the most intense situations. The practice of meditation helps us to recognize and take advantage of these moments of open awareness that occur in the gaps between action and reaction. Once we have cultivated the faculty to see things from a broader perspective, we grow more and more able to experience the gap, or open awareness, even in the middle of an intense argument. Gaps like this provide the opportunity for claustrophobic feelings that come with being trapped in patterns of behavior to give way to feelings of openness and possibility. We can tap into the open awareness that pervades all of our experience to change the course of our actions and ultimately our karmic patterns.

The good news is that while habits may be strong and repetitive, they are also impermanent, and so can be changed.

THREE

The God Realm

TRADITIONAL IMAGERY

The gods occupy the uppermost portion of the wheel. Within the impermanent realms, the gods have achieved the most pleasurable circumstances, ranging from all kinds of physical comforts to mental and spiritual bliss. When in the god realm, our previous efforts, accomplishments, and benevolence have created a world in which much, if not all, of the suffering and inconveniences of life have been removed, or rendered irrelevant.

In the classical Wheel teachings, a stay in the god realms can last for a very long time, even eons. The important point, though, is that however pleasant the experience of the god realm is, it is still temporary. When the causes and conditions of the pleasurable surroundings decay, the heavenly surroundings do too.

It is important to understand that even an afternoon or evening spent in the god realm is subject to impermanence.

Such experiences come and go. Experiencing pleasure is not particularly a problem, and transitoriness in itself is also not a problem. But when we grow attached to pleasurable experiences, then we have problems. Attachment can become the root cause of further suffering, as any recovering addict can tell you.

The god realm has two major aspects. The first is the complete fruition of materialism. When in the god realm state of mind, we can have what we want. There is little or no lag time between desiring something and obtaining it. For many people in the West nowadays, life can be a kind of god realm. Just walk into any supermarket with fifty different kinds of shampoo and you get the picture. We have heating and air conditioning all the time. Our expectation for physical comfort has reached a very high level.

Whether we have conquered the material world or not, another, even higher level of the god realm is when we taste and become infatuated with spiritual bliss. This experience of the god realm—the highest state—is said to be a kind of mental absorption in which we feel infinite ease, comfort, and joy. Some of us who have taken certain psychedelic or other drugs might recognize these states. The meditation high in the god realm may be drug-free, but it still comes with a kind of subtle addiction and attachment to those kinds of carefree mental states.

In the Buddhist teachings spiritual practices that lead to fixation on psychological pleasure and attempt to stabilize blissful states are considered subtle sand traps when compared with the experience of true freedom. We might experience the oneness of everything, the absence of any obstacles, or a cosmic high, but the problem with these states is that although they can last a long time, they are brought about by specific causes and conditions and are therefore impermanent. We think that we have arrived, but we have actually only arrived at an oasis along the long path to awakening.

The problem of the god realm is that we want to sustain that soaring feeling. When we experience relatively blissful states, we feel as if they will last forever. But the truth is that sooner or later we will come down.

THE MINDSET

When we experience the god realm, we base our identity and lifestyle on the experience of pleasure. In this mindset we try to avoid experiencing pain, disappointment, irritation, and discomfort. In trying to extend our experience of the god realm, we have to cultivate a certain kind of ignorance, actively ignoring any aspect of our experience that is unsettling or disruptive to the mood. We don't want there to be the slightest gap in our feelings of bliss.

Given that we experience each of the six realms in a transient way, as discussed above, we cannot spend all of our time in the god realm. It is the nature of the cycle of suffering to constantly rise to the heights of pleasure and then fall to the depths of pain. But most of us have at least experienced moments of bliss and ease at one time or another, even if only on a vacation, a night on the town, or a drug high. In a recent workshop I asked the students if they could relate to the god realm at all and one person volunteered a description of a beautiful sunset dinner at a wonderful restaurant. The food was perfect, the company was great, the setting idyllic. He quickly volunteered that the experience lasted for about five hours, after which he went home, realized he had food poisoning, and spent the rest of the night hugging the porcelain bowl. He had been transported rather swiftly to a minor league version of the hell realm!

One might imagine that if the god realm were an external setting, it would most likely be luxurious, appealing, and orderly, like the student's description of a restaurant with a beautiful lake view at sunset. A more traditional version of that setting could be an extravagant palace or awesome natural landscape. However, the attitude of utter bliss and enjoyment is what really defines the god realm. Even if we live in extremely elegant surroundings and have every physical need met, we may still suffer deep depression, anxiety, or resentment. In that case, even though the external setting may seem superficially like the god realm, our internal experience is much closer to that of the hell realm. If extravagant settings filled with luxury items produce intense and insatiable craving, then our experience of them is more akin to the hungry ghost realm. If such trappings produce competition and jealousy in us, we would be experiencing the mindset of the jealous god realm.

When we feel secure or successful in our work, happy in love, or blissfully submerged in trancelike states of meditation, we are experiencing the god realm. Given the transitory nature of the cycle of suffering, we may even experience god realm bliss in fleeting moments here and there: any time we are just having a perfect day, or even a perfect moment, we are transiting through the god realm.

When we're circling in the experience of the god realm as spiritual practitioners we will likely find it hard to choose between spiritual progress and the intense happiness of worldly bliss and pleasure. The notion of sacrifice or surrender does not come easily in this realm. Our attachment to pleasurable experiences convinces us that there is simply too much to lose.

The idea that one can enjoy both worldly success and spiritual progress is not unusual. It is actually the basis of many advanced Buddhist teachings, including those related to the Shambhala tradition that I have studied for most of my adult life. But if we have too much attachment to pleasure alone, if we hope to preserve the sublime setting of the god realm, it is extremely difficult to truly recognize the impermanence that pervades samsara. If we haven't cultivated this basic realization, it will be very, very hard to let go when it is time for us to go.

It is definitely more excruciating to lose the sublime surroundings, people, and situations we have become attached to, than it is to never to have had them at all. We simply do not recognize the depth and extent of impermanence when we're trapped in a god realm perspective. The fall from heaven when our karma finally runs out is quite painful.

THE PROBLEM

The main obstacle to finding lasting pleasure in the god realm is ignorance of the nature of our experiences there. We fail to really face up to the fact that while we have it good now, things are bound to change; it is inevitable.

Our addiction to pleasurable circumstances leads us to bury our heads in them in order to drown out irritation, disappointment, or the sympathetic pain that comes with caring about the suffering of others.

The blissed out perspective of the god realm biases us toward seeing only those conditions that are positive or pleasurable. Being unable to see the grimmer aspects of reality prevents us from really hearing or being moved by some of life's most powerful messages, such as the pervasiveness of suffering, impermanence, and change. If you've ever had a really pleasant dream and the sound of a garbage truck outside your window woke you up, you understand this obstacle. When we are having a sweet dream, we don't want to wake up—this is true for our night dream and is also true for our daydream.

While it may seem like we've elevated ourselves to the height of spiritual achievement when we attain god realm levels of bliss, from a perspective that takes the entirety of the cycle into consideration, it is clear that we've yet to escape from suffering in any real way. While we delude ourselves with experiences of meditative pleasure, the moments of our lives slip away and we grow no closer to awakening.

THE OPPORTUNITY

We have such a positive perspective in the god realm that we really are in a position to help others. But in order to do that, we have to be able to recognize the difficulties and hardships that others may be facing, even though we ourselves feel perfectly secure. We may relate to feeling that we "just don't want to deal with other people's problems." This is usually an attitude motivated by wanting to preserve our own ease and happiness: it is a god realm perspective. If we were able to risk connecting, to really feel the connection that we all share, whether we are at the peak of happiness or the depths of despair, we would be able to nourish seeds of compassion within ourselves. We have the opportunity to continue to build up our store of positive karma and to benefit others, if we want to.

From the Buddhist point of view, the virtue or good karma that allows us to have god realm experiences is generosity. We can be materially generous or generous in spirit. When things are going so well for us, we are likely in a position to offer support to those around us who may be stuck in a miserable mindset, as in the hell or hungry ghost realms. Being able to genuinely attend to those who are drowning in personal miseries or for whom peace of mind is elusive at the moment is a very meaningful form of generosity that will be beneficial for those around us and ourselves. If, on the other hand, we let our fear of losing our own high allow us to ignore those who suffer around us, we are merely squandering the good karma that brought us that moment of happiness in the first place.

The opportunity that the god realm presents is the opportunity to recognize that the great pleasures that we experience are temporary; they may be the product of virtuous karma, but they are not a reliable refuge from suffering. In a sense, the story of Buddha is the story of a man whose parents attempted to give their son nothing but ideal experiences in life. They hid the realities of old age, sickness, and death—impermanence and suffering—from him for as long as they could.

When their son finally discovered these things for himself, he did not retreat into the safety and security of a life of pleasure, but resolved to face reality head on. In some ways, seeing the impermanent and suffering nature of life from the vantage point of perfect happiness has a greater potential to produce a profound sense of disillusionment. Buddha's initial fall from the experience of the god realm set him squarely on the path to awakening.

THE PRACTICE:
CONTEMPLATING IMPERMANENCE

Contemplation is a specific meditation technique used to explore a particular point of view or experience so as to understand it more completely and develop insight and perspective. It's easy to describe contemplation, but to actually do it takes concentration and discipline. When contemplating we use our thinking mind in a creative way.

To contemplate something, simply attempt to hold your thoughts to a particular topic or feeling, and allow yourself to go deeper and deeper into it. In purposefully contemplating something, we create a more intimate and personal knowledge of the topic being contemplated. By returning to our chosen topic again and again, in a purposeful way, we develop new insights and deeper understanding of it.

When we find ourselves in a god realm mindset, impermanence will be a powerful subject of contemplation. In traditional images of the god realm, a Buddha appears there playing a lute. The lovely note that he plays resonates and decays, communicating to the inhabitants of that realm that even the most pleasurable circumstances are only temporary. All of our experiences are subject to impermanence, even when they are seemingly stable, very pleasurable, and comfortable.

The recognition of this impermanence is what is missing in our god realm perspectives. Attachment to pleasurable states while remaining ignorant of their impermanent nature ultimately brings immense suffering. Paradise lost is more painful than paradise never gained. Contemplating impermanence can wake us up from the daydreams of the god realm, pleasant though they may be.

- Take a good upright posture, sit comfortably in a chair or on a cushion in a quiet place without distractions.
- Begin with a short period of mindfulness meditation: simply note the breath and bodily sensations, settle your mind, and rest it in present awareness.
- Dedicate 5–10 minutes to contemplation.
- Begin by asking yourself a series of questions. You may move through the questions in serial fashion, or select one or two to dwell on.
  - Have I always experienced happiness and pleasure?
  - If my current happiness had a beginning, won't it eventually have an end?
  - What do I ultimately do to myself by

attempting to hold onto current experiences of pleasure, despite knowing, deep down, that they must eventually end?

- Is there anything that is not subject to impermanence and change?
- If I, myself, am constantly changing, who am I really?

Of course, you can formulate any questions you like to help you delve into contemplation on impermanence. The discipline is to hold your mind on this topic.

- If your mind wanders—which it will—simply bring your attention back to the contemplation of impermanence.
- When you come up with a particular question, go deeper into that question.
- After the period dedicated to contemplation comes to an end, rest your mind and let the whole exploration naturally dissolve.
- End with a short period of mindfulness meditation: simply note the breath and bodily sensations, settle your mind, and rest it in present awareness.

This kind of contemplation helps us to develop deeper insight into our experiences and the ability to discern between how things appear, how we wish them to be, and how they actually are. Contemplation like this can help us become disillusioned in a positive sense; they free us from illusion. If we recognize the truth of impermanence and understand that we tend to grasp at fleeting realities, even though our world is always shifting and changing, we have an easier time shifting our perspective and letting go. These types of shift in perspective, opening the mind, are the whole point of studying the Wheel and practicing meditation.

FOUR

The Jealous God Realm

TRADITIONAL IMAGERY

According to traditional depictions, the realm of the jealous gods is dominated by envy and competition. As in the god realm, beings are born into the jealous god realm because of good karma from previous lives. However, unlike the gods, the jealous gods do not have confidence that their situation is sustainable. They therefore find themselves living in a world of paranoia, jealousy, relentless competition, and one-upmanship. Power and control are the currency of the jealous god realm. The jealous gods are constantly warring amongst themselves and launching attacks on the gods—though they never defeat them—to maintain and improve their status. They may have position and respect, but their perch is too precarious to be stable, and they expend a lot of energy to establish and maintain it.

THE MINDSET

When we are envious or competitive, preoccupied with surpassing others in some way, we definitely know the jealous gods' state of mind. It is as though we are climbing to the top of a human heap and the only way to get there is to clamber over others and push them to the bottom. Even when we find ourselves on the top of the heap, we must defend our position against those fighting to take our place. We cannot trust that we will keep the position we achieve amid a dynamic field of competitors. It is important for us to win the game, but it must be equally important that others lose.

The price of our position is constant vigilance. We must have eyes in back of our heads to make sure nobody is going to undermine our position or surpass us in whatever we are pursuing. We are constantly plotting and maneuvering to maintain our status.

It seems that no aspect of life is free from this scheming. Clubs to which we belong, where we eat, where we shop, the clothes we wear, the car we drive, all represent status and achievement as much as a standard of living. Friends, lovers, even family can become tools or trophies in the competitive mindset. We choose our friends for all kinds of reasons, but one of those reasons may be the advantage they afford us, or simply how they reflect on us. While we may also concern ourselves with the quality of our children's education, we may be influenced to select their school based on its prestige. Within every situation, it seems, there is the possibility for competition.

When we are experiencing the jealous god realm, we favor competition over collaboration. When we compare ourselves to those around us—even those closest to us—in order to gauge where we stand in the pecking order, we are experiencing the mindset of a jealous god. In this mindset our current status, no matter what it is, will never really be sufficient or satisfying. We always want more and will always seek to get it.

Like the gods we may have a life of relative ease and comfort, but we also fear losing it. We try to create desirable circumstances for ourselves, but our enjoyment of them is undermined by the jealous god's desire to upgrade, so there is no real ease, relaxation, or contentment. We could recognize impermanence in the tenuous nature of our position, but we fall prey again to insecurity before we can reap the benefits.

It may be easiest to imagine this realm in terms of material success, but as with all of the realms, it is really a mindset. A scuffle at work can manifest the game of competition, put-downs, and manipulation, but so can a flare-up of sibling rivalry. We can also perhaps get a little too competitive playing on a community softball team, or begin to feel anxious if a good friend seems to prefer spending time with someone else. We may not see it at first glance, but we have many different roles and positions in life and so the potential for competition is everywhere.

Anytime we become preoccupied with assessing the competition and maintaining or expanding our personal power, we are cycling through the jealous god realm. Being in the jealous god realm does not depend on a particular sphere of life; anyone can be swept away by the desire to advance, to look good, to be the best, most talented, or most powerful. Whenever we become emotionally invested in competition, either worrying over our own position or desiring a better one, we are visiting the jealous god realm. We're all familiar with such experiences, although it may be easier to see in others.

THE PROBLEM

The main obstacle to finding balance or peace in the jealous god realm is an ongoing sense of paranoia derived from constant competition. When we consider our own progress and how it measures up, we cannot be truly satisfied, no matter what we may have accomplished. It is difficult to develop compassion when dominated by such a mindset. As we struggle to make or maintain progress, we find little room in our hearts for others, unless caring for them somehow serves our own agenda. We end up cutting ourselves off from others when we get swallowed up in our own drama, thinking of them only in terms of how they fit into our narrative. We grow so sharp that we can't even see the value of tenderness when circumstance calls for such feelings.

After all, we only make ourselves look good in comparison to someone else. One side wins only at the expense of the other. As such, the jealous god frame of mind doesn't really foster concern for the well-being of others. "If the competition doesn't realize the way of the world, too bad for them and all the better for me." From this perspective, dealing with somebody who is kind and generous is like taking candy from a baby.

It is most difficult to keep intimate relationships in this space. When we feel very protective of our own interests and would do almost anything to protect them, it's very hard to believe that others don't feel the same about theirs. How can we feel a true connection with someone else when we only think in terms of our own self-interest?

When swallowed up by a jealous god mindset, even spiritual pursuits may be directed toward increasing our sense of control over our environment and those in it. If we flaunt our spirituality, or espouse religious teachings in order to feel or look superior, we are in the jealous god mentality. This mentality can be a dangerous trap for powerfully creative and talented people, even those with spiritual leanings. We may delude ourselves with the sense of superiority that comes with competition and victory, but we actually grow farther from enlightenment as we grow more and more hardened to the lot of others.

THE OPPORTUNITY

We tend to get things done when in a jealous god mindset, and in this sense we really could make progress if we could get past the self-involvement that comes with the perspective. Each of the realms has qualities embedded within it that can be transformed if we can strip away its self-centered, neurotic aspects. From the jealous god perspective, we have a profound sense of clarity and are able to fearlessly take action. Unfortunately, these qualities are completely tinged with a strong sense of envy and competition, and so are unable to be as useful to us as they would otherwise be.

We did not achieve whatever gains we have made in life by accident. We have made deliberate decisions and done some hard work. We really show this kind of industriousness when experiencing the jealous god realm. Our minds grow sharp and active. We are not afraid to take action and manifest our ideas in the world. In fact we prefer to be engaged. If the sharpness and intelligence we experience in this mindset can be conjoined with compassion rather than with competition, we will clearly recognize that our well-being is intimately intertwined with the well-being of others.

We have a powerful feeling of moving situations forward and achieving goals when in the jealous god state. If we can strip away the self-referential need for assurance, control, and dominance, we can use the skills of being organized, motivated, skillful at seeing what is called for, and able to get things done in a more compassionate way.

The jealous god realm presents the opportunity to truly experience humility and surrender, elements that are crucial to any kind of genuine learning. Confronting and going through adverse situations, like defeat or loss of prestige, offer us the chance to really connect with others and to cultivate empathy and compassion. The intense feeling of suffering that comes with loss of status can itself become a cause of identifying with the suffering of others. Recognizing that self-involvement makes this misery worse also encourages us to be less self-involved and more considerate of others. If we can recognize the jealous god mindset for what it is and resist the temptation to gear up and go once more into the fray, we can become less aggressive and goal-driven, while still keeping our edge, clarity, and knack for getting things done.

THE PRACTICE:
CULTIVATING COMPASSION

When we are stuck in an envious, competitive mindset, developing a healthy recognition of connection with others and seeing the benefit of including them in our larger goal of fulfillment and well-being can transform our experience into something valuable.

The practice of *tonglen*, or "giving and taking," is a traditional Buddhist meditation that focuses the mind and brings out our compassion for others. The practice unfolds in four stages and can be practiced at any time.

1. Begin by taking a moment to glimpse the inherent feeling of being open and awake right on the spot. Experience yourself and your environment exactly as they are in this very moment, for a moment, and then let it go.

2. Call to mind the basic abstract quality of suffering: a hot, dark, heavy, and claustrophobic feeling. Visualize that you breathe this suffering in as a heavy smog. Imagine that you fully draw the black cloud of suffering into your body. Here you practice fearlessness by taking on whatever negativities are around you, rather than repressing or avoiding them. So, as you breathe suffering in, maintain a

fearless, open attitude, without rejecting suffering or trying to protect yourself from it. Obviously this approach is radical and unconventional.

Next call to mind the basic abstract quality of happiness and bliss: light, cooling, positive, and refreshing. As you breathe out, visualize that happiness and bliss radiate out from your nose, mouth, and skin in the form of radiant white light. A positive, expansive, loving feeling pours out of you to all beings. As you breathe in and out, practice taking on suffering of others and giving all of your happiness to them in concert with your in and out breaths, respectively.

3. Once you have established basic giving and taking in concert with your breath, think of someone who is suffering right now and can use some help. Their situation is real, moving, and you want to personally help them. Send out your best feelings to them on each exhale. On each inhalation take on and take in any pain and suffering they are currently experiencing, just like a parent would do for their child. When you are comfortable with giving and taking with respect to one person, expand the scope of your practice to include anybody else who is suffering in a similar way, even yourself if that feels appropriate.

If you are stuck, do the practice for yourself and simultaneously for all those like you who are suffering in a particular way. For instance if you are working with depression, you breathe that feeling in for yourself and all others who might be also working with depression and send out your relief in whatever form feels right, synchronized with the outbreath.

4. Lastly, try to extend the practice as widely as you can, perhaps including others or even all the people who might be suffering in a similar way as the person upon whom you are focusing. For example, if you are thinking of a friend who has cancer, you could imagine that you are breathing in and out for all people who are suffering from cancer. You are connecting your heart to theirs.

When you are ready to end your session of giving and taking, return your awareness to the present, settle your mind on the breath and the sensation of it in the body, and let your efforts dissolve. The feeling of exchanging yourself for others may linger after practice, and that is fine.

When you practice giving and taking in the field, simply breathe in the difficulty and pain of the other person and breathe out a sense of spaciousness and relief, right there as the exchange is happening. Obviously other people do not need to know what you are doing for the practice to work.

Giving and taking is a simple, but very deep and in some sense challenging, meditation. It cuts directly into the self-involved, fearful, and competitive mindset of the jealous god realm. When our minds are in the jealous god realm, we are sharp and powerful but find it very difficult to be truly open to the pain and suffering of others. So we may feel isolated and cut off. As we open our heart to others, we are also increasing our compassion for ourselves and can become more accepting of our own frailties and imperfections. In some sense the practice makes us more human: by doing it, we actually move back into a human realm mindset. We might feel less powerful, dominating, and in control, but our heart opens and blood once again flows through it.

FIVE

The Human Realm

TRADITIONAL IMAGERY

We live the traditional imagery of the human realm: we are born, we die, we study, work, and have families. This may all seem ordinary and run-of-the-mill, but the human realm is actually quite poignant and filled with passion. We denizens of the human realm understand how fragile and impermanent life really is. We experience birth, then the joys and sorrows of youth, and then ultimately old age, sickness, and death. We experience both pleasure and pain, which alternate in such a way that we never really settle too deeply into either. This fluctuation between pleasure and pain is what makes humans feel open and vulnerable. From the traditional perspective, the human realm is special because it is primarily in this realm that one has access to the Buddha and his teachings of the awakened mind. Being born as a human in a healthy body in a place where one can receive spiritual teachings and evolve is traditionally considered most auspicious.

The Buddhist tradition provides many analogies that express the rarity of this opportunity. A well-known analogy asks us to imagine a shoreless sea on which a golden yoke drifts about, tossed here and there by the waves. In this sea lives a tortoise that only surfaces once every thousand years. To be born as a human is said to be as rare as the likelihood of that turtle's neck passing through the opening of the yoke when it surfaces. Our human lives are considered rare and precious, free and well favored, and we are encouraged not to waste them.

THE MINDSET

The mindset of the human realm may be the most transparent and undetectable of all the realms. To become aware of our human realm perspective is like a fish trying to see the water in which it swims.

Because the experience of the human realm alternates so frequently between pleasure and pain, we constantly long for what has passed, plan for what may come, worry about how things will go, aspire to change ourselves, and explore new options. The human realm perspective is the most discursive of all the realms. When experiencing this mindset, we are almost always chasing some train of thought, often with more randomness and unpredictability than we would like. This kind of mind is sometimes called "frog mind," because it leaps around so much. In Tibetan it is called *kuntag*, meaning "random fixation." Our minds just jump around from topic to topic and fixate on each for a relatively short period of time. Then, without rhyme or reason, we jump to another topic, perhaps prompted by a loose association or a flash of anxiety about some future event.

Our relationship with our hearts and feelings are powerfully swayed by this state. It is the realm of passion and so also the realm of potential for compassion. The human perspective allows us to easily experience sympathy and empathy for others. We can feel sympathy for all beings or at least for specific groups of beings we care about. The feelings that we hold for others can even break our hearts. In a real sense, the vacillation between pleasure and pain that comes with being human is also what makes us sensitive to the suffering of others.

In an effort to alleviate uncertainty about our situation, we look for answers and solutions to the big questions in life. The uncertainty that comes with being human opens us to exploring our world in new ways. The human perspective gives birth to religion, philosophy, inquiry, and deep curiosity concerning the nature of the world. In this mindset we read and write, ask for and offer guidance, and seek shared experiences as a ground on which to cultivate friendships and community.

We are generating our own storylines, but at the same time we are interested in the stories of others. We are curious about what makes others tick, even when we don't like them. Perhaps they had a difficult childhood or a problem with substance abuse. Maybe they're just having a really bad day. We find ourselves looking deeper before we judge others too harshly, because it is easy to see ourselves in their place. We seek to understand others as much as we seek to understand ourselves. The potential for compassion rests within this impulse to share and learn with other human beings.

That is why the Buddha appeared to us as an ordinary human being who presented the facts of life—the Dharma—in a straightforward and relatable way. Our teacher is somebody who lived the same kind of life that we live, related to the same kinds of obstacles and challenges that we do, and learned to transform all of them into a path of wisdom and compassion. Because we are human, we seek out and learn from such teachers.

THE PROBLEM

We have a tremendous opportunity to learn and grow here, but we spend much of our time stuck on the treadmill of life, trying to get by, to just make it through another day, to make it to retirement. Then, before we know it, the years go by, we get old, sick, and then die. A kind of habitual sleepiness that attaches itself primarily to the fulfillment of the mundane aspects of our existence is mixed in with the potential that the human realm perspective has for awakening.

The drama of the human realm comes from the fact that the potential for enlightenment exists side by side with the comfort of life in samsara. We are attracted to the idea of just managing our apparent reality without ever really penetrating through to the realization of our full individual potential.

In the midst of our passions, our joys, and suffering, we receive invitation after invitation to wake up, to open our hearts fully to ourselves and others, and to contribute to our fellow creatures. But we often choose the path of least resistance, find comfort in our habitual patterns, and are content to watch the clock wind down. The human realm has the most contrast, the most opportunity, and the most insidious subtle obstacles of all.

THE OPPORTUNITY

Life in the human realm has the most potential for complete awakening. The human realm experience of empathy gives us a great opportunity to develop limitless kindness, compassion, and wisdom. The human realm mindset is truly precious, because it offers us the best opportunity to achieve liberation from the six realms altogether.

The human realm offers up myriad opportunities to fully experience life. The awakened state is said to be none other than fully experiencing our life in this very moment. Many great teachers have pointed to this kind of direct and present experience as the essence of realization.

Meditation is the method by which we refocus our awareness on the present and simply note and release all of the memories and anticipations that perpetually flood our mind and disturb our emotions and bodily sensations. Meditation allows us to get to know ourselves exactly as we are and to open a gateway to awakening from within our daydream right here and now. Each time we sit down to practice meditation, and then again when we experience the world more mindfully, we can awaken from our daydream.

This shift of attention, tuning in to our natural wakefulness, is very possible when in a human realm mindset. Many others have managed to do it, and we have all the equipment we need to do it too. Having this opportunity pointed out by a teacher, book, mentor, or friend can be a significant turning point in one's life. Once we realize the potential we have, we can begin to gradually move beyond our feelings of stagnation, blame, ambivalence, and laziness, and begin to cultivate a more awakened life. This is clearly the opportunity of the human realm.

THE PRACTICE:
MINDFULNESS MEDITATION

Mindfulness is a great starting point for meditation practice and is the core foundation for many other practices you might undertake. It is also a complete practice in itself with significant and tangible benefits.

1. TAKE YOUR SEAT
   Begin by taking your meditation seat, usually in a stable, cross-legged position on a cushion on the floor. You'll want to get into a comfortable posture with a good firm connection between your butt and the cushion. You should feel grounded and stable. Then you can just rest your hands on your thighs or your knees.

   Your torso, head, and shoulders should be upright but relaxed. Gently tuck your chin in a bit so your head does not jut forward. The posture should feel dignified and upright, but not stiff or tense. The general guideline is "not too tight and not too loose," and that is good advice throughout.

If you have trouble sitting cross-legged for whatever reason, you can take a kneeling posture or just sit upright on a chair. Use any kind of support you need (cushions, etc.) to be comfortable. But whatever position you assume, your back should be as straight as possible and not supported by a wall or the back of a chair, unless it's absolutely necessary.

A good, stable posture produces a feeling of containment and reduces our sphere of activity. Make sure your jaw is relaxed and slightly open. Your eyes should be open with a soft downward gaze, resting about four to six feet on the floor in front of you. Do not shut down your awareness of the space around you, but do relax your visual focus.

2. PLACE YOUR ATTENTION ON THE BREATH

Having settled your body in this way, begin to pay attention to your breath as it moves in and out. You can place your attention on the breath, at the tip of the nose, on the feeling of the stomach rising and falling, or just feel the entire flow of breath in and out of your body. Do not attempt to manipulate your breath; just breathe normally. As you pay attention, your awareness will naturally become connected to your breath. This doesn't require intense focus. Simply maintain a relaxed attentiveness to the breath as it goes in and out of your body.

Sometimes you will notice that your awareness has drifted. You may end up thinking about your relationship, your work week coming up, or your next meal. Regardless of your thoughts, when you find your focus has drifted away from the breath, gently bring your attention back to your breath without any kind of comment or evaluation. Just bring it back.

3. LABEL THOUGHTS AS THINKING

When you notice that you're thinking, just say to yourself, "Thinking." Just label it with that one word, and then gently bring your attention back to your breath. Trungpa Rinpoche used to say that when you are sitting like this, you have a flat bottom and your thoughts also have a flat bottom. Before, maybe your thoughts were all over the place and were taking you with them, but now your body is settled and your mental activity will gradually settle down as well.

It is also helpful to recognize that, in some sense, all of our thoughts are equal. Do not favor some thoughts or freak out about others. Very simply, when you notice you are thinking and have drifted away from awareness of the breath, just label any and all thoughts "thinking" and bring your attention back to the breath. You are neither repressing your thoughts, nor are you following them. You are simply letting them be as they are, noticing them, and returning your attention to your breath.

If you grow uncomfortable or need to move to restore circulation during longer periods of sitting, bring your legs up in front of your chest and continue your practice. Once your legs feel comfortable and circulation has been restored, just resettle yourself into your posture and begin again.

It's OK to begin modestly at first, maybe sitting for about ten to fifteen minutes in three to four sessions per week. From there you can build up to a daily sitting practice for however long feels right for you.

Meditating is an excellent use of our time as human beings here on planet Earth. It is like coming home to who we truly are. It is a beautiful, powerful, and rewarding expression of our human nature.

SIX

The Animal Realm

TRADITIONAL IMAGERY

Traditionally the animal realm refers to animals, both wild and those in close relationship to our human world, ranging from the ants crawling outside your house, to deer and bears, fish and birds, down to your favorite toy poodle. Some of us might romanticize the experience of being an animal. Of course animals are intuitive creatures that live simply, in harmony with nature, but imagine spending your whole day trying to catch food or trying to not become food and you might quickly change your mind.

The main quality of the animal realm is ignorance. In it we are focused on tried and true paths toward pleasure and away from pain. We develop myriad sticky habits, repeating whatever has brought us comfort and avoiding any situations that are uncertain or threatening to our established patterns. In the traditional imagery, we act just like a pig with blinders, following deeply ingrained patterns of behavior in a rigid and predictable way, eating our way through whatever is right in front of us. Life in the animal realm is mindlessly relying on habit to bring us pleasure and keep us from pain.

THE MINDSET

One day when I was studying with Trungpa Rinpoche, a large number of inchworms covered the pathway to his house in Berkeley. We students were asked to be careful not to harm them on our way in and out. I sat watching one of them methodically working its way across a table, hunching its little body up and then straightening it out again, slowly but surely inching its way closer to its destination.

Just then Rinpoche's senior student came walking by. I asked him if he understood the teachings on the Wheel of Life to mean that one of us human beings could actually reincarnate as one of those little inchworms. Without missing a beat he simply said, "You know how that feels." I did indeed. I think we all do.

In the animal realm mindset all of the analysis we experience in the human realm is dumbed down in order to create the illusion of a safe and predictable world. Our mentality becomes deliberate and plodding, like that little inchworm, and quite dull with respect to making any change to routines. We fall into behaviors from the past that were useful, even when the situation has changed and they are no longer effective. We tell ourselves, "We do it this way because we always do it this way" and blindly follow the rules. Even if we rebel against the rules, it is only in a very predictable way. We can see this happen in every aspect of our lives: we wake up at the same time each day, choose the same foods and clothes, do the same work, and have the same interactions with our co-workers and loved ones. We settle into repeatable routines to avoid experiencing uncertainty.

When in the animal realm mindset, we enshrine our routines as a saving grace, and much of our passion and inquisitiveness is stifled to increase our comfort level. Apart from the routines of life mentioned above, our routines could also be internal. For instance we find ourselves unquestioningly clinging to old, familiar feelings, beliefs, or ideas, as a matter of course. Or we could open ourselves to potentially harmful situations merely because they feel familiar. We find ourselves arguing social or political positions that we're not certain we believe. Pleasant family traditions become old habits and spiritual practices become mindless rituals. All kinds of acts, when done mindlessly, come to embody the deadening quality of the animal realm.

The animal realm mentality narrows down the options, diminishes the need for inquiry and exploration, and creates a regulated and stale environment around us. The key obstacle—which is ironically similar to that of the god realm—is ignorance, or ignoring the dynamic, fluid, changeable nature of our experience. It is simply too uncertain and anxiety-provoking to build our operation on that kind of unstable platform. The animal realm mind is our reliance on stability.

THE PROBLEM

The main obstacle we face in the animal realm is the absence of curiosity or discernment. Our patterns are so thick and so well established that we rarely question who we are, what we are doing, or what else might be possible. The questioning mind is key to cultivating a sense of inquiry and growth, but in the animal realm comfort trumps investigation. We are stuck in a fog of habitual patterns.

Ironically it is partly our experience of discomfort that creates the opportunity to learn and grow. In the animal realm we tend to avoid discomfort and we can be very shut down when it comes to engaging fresh situations that require us to open our minds and absorb new information. In the animal realm it is difficult to think in a way that might change our situation significantly. We can become stuck in a quagmire of fixed beliefs about all kinds of things.

A very defensive stance also accompanies this mentality. Defending fixed beliefs can drop us into a fight or flight mode. Our drive to defend our illusions of security can lead us to resist change, either by lashing out at or fleeing from, any challenge to our established patterns. Compromise is not an option: any compromise to the routine is still change.

Any learning in the animal realm is totally utilitarian. Our attitude is to know just what we need to know to survive and preserve the status quo. The greatest challenge for us when we are in the animal realm mindset is to dredge up some motivation and curiosity to explore our world and ourselves in order to see their potential.

THE OPPORTUNITY

In the animal realm, we have the opportunity to really get in touch with the earthy aspects of our existence. We are grounded in the practical realities of our physical being. Every day we eat, sleep, create stability, and survive. On the one hand this can produce a dense thicket of ritual behavior, but it can also tune us in to the practicalities and basic urges of our daily lives.

Although we experience a torpor of complacency in the animal realm that keeps our sense of inquiry in check, there is also a kind of wisdom of dealing with the basics: the concrete, non-theoretical aspect of our existence. We all need to pay attention to the practical aspects of our lives. How will we secure our food, water, and shelter and protect our families and communities? These capabilities are well developed in the animal realm. There can even be a sense of power and strength in dealing with everyday life that is admirable and desirable.

If we can muster some discriminating awareness and inquiry into our sense of self, we can elevate our thought process and move ourselves closer toward the human realm mindset. The opportunity the animal realm mindset affords is that it allows us to experience and know our strong, protected base, and thereby, to destabilize our powerfully embedded habitual routines, just enough to allow for new exploration and growth to happen.

THE PRACTICE: INSIGHT MEDITATION

The purpose of insight meditation is to cultivate panoramic awareness, to develop the ability to see our minds and experiences unfold with impartiality and precision. To achieve this goal, we must cultivate what is sometimes called the *witness* or *impartial watcher*. We can examine our experience as it arises with an open, unbiased awareness, boycotting knee-jerk reactivity, judgment, and bias.

The practice of insight is a logical extension of the mindfulness meditation we explored in the chapter on the human realm. So by extending our meditation practice and making it more inclusive of all the experiences that arise in our awareness, we can use the stable platform that we developed with basic mindfulness meditation and extend it to develop awareness and insight into the nature of our experience altogether.

- Begin by taking a good, strong seat, cross-legged on a cushion or sitting upright on a chair. Draw your attention to the breath flowing in and out of your body. As with mindfulness meditation, you can place your attention on the breath at the tip of the nose, on the feeling of the stomach rising and falling, or just feel the entire flow of breath in and out of your body.

- Again, when you notice that you are thinking about something else—anything else—simply label the thoughts "thinking," and bring your attention back to the breath.

- When practicing insight meditation, do not simply

drop thoughts and physical sensations that arise. Instead, take note of them with a light touch of awareness and actually feel the texture of those experiences.

- Observe your thoughts, emotions, and sensations, and attempt to see them clearly, as they are, in the moment. If you feel hungry, explore the feeling further. What exactly does it feel like? Where does hunger actually occur? Is there a feeling in your belly, in your throat, in your mind maybe?

- If emotions arise, take note of them—anger, jealousy, pride, resentment—and simply feel their impact on your mind and body. Actually pay attention, without too much analysis, to the experiences that arise while you are meditating; at the same time, keep a bare thread of attention on your breath to ground the exercise.

- End the session by returning your awareness to the breath and settling into the moment again.

When beginning insight meditation, we will notice that our attention is divided to explore four aspects of our experience. One part of our attention focuses on awareness of the breath. A second part takes note of the thoughts going through our minds, without rejecting, dwelling on, or manipulating them further. A third part watches our sense perceptions: the sounds of the room we are in, the quality of the light, the feeling of the breeze on our skin, the smell of the bakery next door, and so on. And lastly, a fourth part of our attention just remains open and relaxed. This is, of course, a very general outline meant to illustrate how attention is more distributed in the practice of insight meditation.

Cultivating a more panoramic style of awareness keeps us alert without fixating on any particular stimulus, like the breath. In the animal realm, we tend to lock onto particular experiences, simplistically viewing them as either good or bad without being open to all the possibilities in between. Practicing insight meditation expands our awareness and opens us to new perspectives and possibilities. It can definitely break up the fogginess of our minds when we're in an animal realm mindset.

SEVEN

The Hungry Ghost Realm

TRADITIONAL IMAGERY

In the traditional imagery, hungry ghosts are beings who—due to their accumulation of negative karma—are stuck in a place where they crave voraciously, but can never, ever get satisfaction. They are portrayed as starving wraiths with tiny mouths, thin necks, and very large bellies, all of which symbolizes their insatiable hunger. The hungry ghost realm can be seen as a metaphor for an addictive personality. In this mindset we are ceaselessly plagued by hunger and thirst but can never take in enough of what we crave to satisfy our desire.

THE MINDSET

All of our minds have visited the hungry ghost realm. We have all tasted this kind of insatiability in one area of our lives or another. Have you ever been lonely, stressed out, or anxious and reached for a drink, a snack, some affirmation of worth, while at the same time feeling that whatever you grab cannot possibly fill the hole? If the answer is yes, then you have visited the hungry ghost realm. When we are in the mindset of the hungry ghost, we experience constant craving and are never satisfied. We desperately seek food, drink, recognition, love, and so on. The experience of contentment is always just beyond our grasp and slips away as we reach for it.

The hungry ghost realm is wherever we find ourselves unconsciously reaching for or consciously scrambling after that one thing that will make us whole. It does not even exist solely in our actions; often, even if we're not acting on our addiction, we're thinking about acting on it. Anybody who has had an even mildly dependent relationship with something—caffeine, nicotine, food, another person—understands that sometimes our cravings seem beyond our control. It's as if, even absent of our minds, our bodies are saying, "I actually need this."

What defines this realm, however, is the repetitive, obsessive, relentless, and urgent quality of our neediness. When we crave like this, there is a blinding urgency that comes over us that will not be denied. But we are not talking only about illegal drugs, or their more socially acceptable counterparts; our craving can be for any little thing. In this mindset, nothing will ever suffice: we will never have enough love, enough money, the right things, or the right lifestyle to make us happy.

You might think that we could recognize our empty cravings by all of the disappointment they cause. But in the hungry ghost mindset, our craving distorts our perceptions such that we are blind to the fact that indulgence will not satisfy us. If we eat, drink, or smoke too much, for example, we might wake up sick. But the next time the opportunity to imbibe presents itself we develop amnesia. We rationalize that the sickness was just bad luck, or bad judgment; this time will be better. Not even pain or sickness deters our desire.

As with all of the other realms, the hungry ghost mindset affects us regardless of our physical circumstances. Even in a luxurious, seemingly god-realm type of environment, we could still experience tremendous craving and dissatisfaction. Given any everyday situation—a meal with family or friends, something we are doing for work, or how we spend an evening alone—someone in a hungry ghost mindset is never satisfied with what they have and, no matter how far they pursue the object of their desire, they are never happy with what they get. In those hungry ghost moments, nothing will satisfy us.

THE PROBLEM

The problem with acting like a hungry ghost is that the constant anxiety we feel over our dissatisfaction leaves no room for proper appreciation or for the development of perspective. The hungry ghost mindset upsets our clarity. Like all of the other states, it recurs relentlessly. Perhaps more than in any other realm, our psychology powerfully reinforces our habits of cravings with feelings of emptiness.

This vast and deep feeling of emptiness, a void that inspires panic and dread, drives our craving. Additionally, our neediness can become somaticized (as in addiction), so we actually feel like our body is dragging us deeper and deeper into the realm experience. Ironically, there is actually no solid, reliable, or satisfying essence within the objects of our craving. Even if we get what we want, it doesn't have the power to satisfy us completely. So we panic and chase after the next object, thinking it will be the magic cure for our emptiness and longing.

THE OPPORTUNITY

With practice we can cultivate the insight that the object of our craving and the craving itself are not as substantial as they superficially seem. We suspect that there must be more to life than the endless round of desire, chase, acquire, and tire.

Many of us have had some experience in the hungry ghost realm. We might be able to see, on a good day, that the solid fixation on our projections is fundamentally empty of any permanent substance; it is, however, a deeply ingrained habit. Of course when we are deep in the grips of some burning desire, it is quite difficult to see its empty nature. The overwhelming want that we experience convinces us that the object of our craving will really satisfy us, if only we can get it. But once we recognize that we are in the grip of an obsessive craving, the opportunity to undermine its power also presents itself.

When we come face to face with insatiable craving, we are nearly face to face with the emptiness that drives it. When we are confronted with the fact that our desire never really abates no matter how much we get, we are being presented with the opportunity to clearly see a truth about the nature of the cycle of existence. In this sense, finding ourselves plagued with a hungry ghost mindset and "hitting the bottom" in that realm may be the beginning of our disillusionment with the whole samsaric charade. This is perhaps why recovering addicts often move toward some form of spiritual practice—so they can stabilize and deepen that recognition.

THE PRACTICE: CULTIVATING GENEROSITY

In general the approach to meditation in the six realms is to cultivate that which is in short supply. When you find yourself in the hungry ghost realm, you are feeling poverty-stricken and without resources. You cannot extend generosity either toward yourself or others, so it's natural that the antidote will be to cultivate material, as well as emotional, generosity.

Traditionally, we can cultivate several kinds of generosity:

1. Material generosity: You can simply give something to others or even to yourself—food, clothing, money, shelter, and so on. Donating to charity or working in a food kitchen are examples of material generosity. Generosity toward yourself is also important. Buying yourself some good food, or taking a trip you've wanted to take, can be expressions of this kind of attitude. The important point is moving toward contentment, which is exactly what is missing. So if you do give the gift of material generosity you should be mindful about not

creating further craving and dissatisfaction in the process.

2. The gift of fearlessness: Lurking behind your impoverished mentality is fear. You are afraid you are inadequate, not good enough in some way, so you grasp at external comfort and superficial confirmation to generate a feeling of adequacy. If you can cultivate the bravery to uproot those deep-seated feelings of inadequacy and help others to do the same, you give the gift of fearlessness.

   Significantly, in many Twelve Step programs, mentoring others can become a strong part of one's own evolution and practice. Helping others to face their underlying fears and anxieties can help you strengthen your compassion and resolve to work with your own fears.

3. The gift of Dharma: Dharma means seeing things clearly as they are. The truth is that we are fundamentally good and whole human beings. We may have layers and layers of doubt and insecurity, but at the root, at the core, we are basically good. We can experience contentment, appreciation, and respect for ourselves and others. We can cultivate stability and go beyond the constant need for confirmation and external approval.

   Because the habit of craving and cherishing is so strong, we may need to develop further insight into the nature of our suffering. Mindfulness and insight meditation practices can help us see our patterns more clearly and create a space between craving and grasping, which is the most important link in the vicious cycle that generates the hungry ghost mentality.

It might be helpful to note here that some aspects of our practice are more formal, like the mindfulness, insight, and contemplative meditations. These are done in a quiet space, taking a good upright sitting posture. Others, like being generous, compassionate, kind, mindful, and aware (in the "field") are more informal; we practice them at any time in the course of our everyday lives. These types of practices are where formal practice pays off by infusing our minds and hearts as we engage our world.

EIGHT

The Hell Realm

TRADITIONAL IMAGERY

The possibility of any kind of pleasure whatsoever has completely receded in the hell realm. There, existence has been completely overwhelmed by the experience of pain and suffering. Traditional iconography depicts a variety of hell realms, which are generally divided into hot and cold hells. Hot hells are filled with hatred and violence. In these realms, beings are flayed alive, have molten lead poured down their throats, and are beaten unconscious by terrifying demons, before being revived and beaten again. Cold hells are frozen wastelands with no warmth or sustenance in sight. In these realms, beings are exposed to the bitter, unimaginable cold, until their bodies freeze, their skin cracks open, and they eventually shatter into pieces, before being revived and going through the process all over again. The emotional landscape of hell is nothing but feelings of imprisonment, terrifying fear, silent rage, and hopelessness. In the hell realms, anguish and pain are relentless.

THE MINDSET

The experience of the hell realm is dominated by feelings of aggression toward others and disgust with ourselves. A hell realm mindset is characterized by bouts of uncontrollable anger or depression. Anger can leap explosively out of us when we fall into a hell realm state of mind. Or it may fester and simmer behind a silent wall of rage. From this point of view, we find it easy to find fault with others, blaming them for our misery and pain. But the expression of a hellish mental state needn't be physically aggressive. We may take a passive aggressive tack, trying to sneak in some kind of revenge without confronting anyone directly. The motives underlying expressions of hell realm mentality are totally toxic.

Sometimes the hell realm psychology turns inward, and we take ourselves as the object of ridicule and resentment. Certainly we've all had a black day where we feel completely trapped in negativity: "I suck. My life sucks. Everything sucks." It's as if a shroud falls over everything, and we cannot see anything positive about life. Sometimes this type of self-loathing gloom can get so bad that we can't even get out of bed. Anyone who has suffered depression will acknowledge that it is a type of hell.

The hell realm mindset is the polar opposite of the god realm mindset. There, we are always high, everything is great, and life is beautiful; here, we are always low, everything is terrible, and life is as ugly as it can get. Just as we don't give a second thought to the possibility that our good luck will run out when in the middle of a heavenly experience, we just cannot see any possible end to our misery when swallowed up by a hellish one. The hell realm mindset sees everything in the extreme.

THE PROBLEM

The biggest problem we face when overwhelmed by a hell realm mindset is that we cannot see any possibility that things will change. Hellish experiences feel like dead ends in every sense of the word. The person we hate will always be terrible, the life we dislike will always be utterly disappointing, or the depression and isolation we feel will never fade. When things are at their worst, we may even contemplate violence, murder, or suicide—extreme solutions for impossible problems.

The cycle of negative emotions leading to negative expectations leading to negative outcomes fuels itself. The overwhelming nature of hell realm experiences make it difficult to foresee getting a fresh start, new input, relief, or resolution. Hopelessness and despair prevent us from understanding that such intense experiences are, like all others, fleeting and impermanent. Our view of the impermanence of our current situation is completely obstructed. Even if we meet a wise teacher or friend who is capable of showing us how our perspective traps us, the hell realm mindset may prevent us from really hearing them. When our minds are completely submerged in anger and resentment, we are more apt to treat genuine gestures of care or helpfulness with cynicism or outright disdain: "You

couldn't possibly understand what I'm going through."
Once we've succumbed to a hell realm mentality, it can be
very difficult to free ourselves from the cycle of negativity
that it produces.

THE OPPORTUNITY

The abject misery that we experience in the hell realm
mindset offers us the opportunity to relate to the suffering
of others. We can look at the depths of the unhappiness
that come with our own hellish experiences and recognize
that no one wants to feel this way. It is a terrible way to go
through even one day of life: isolated, angry, utterly help-
less to change it, and with no end in sight. If we are able
to rouse ourselves enough to recognize that we have fallen
under the sway of a particular state of mind, we can also
see how those we may hate are likewise subject to such
experiences.

This isn't to say that we simply forgive the harmful
behavior of others. Instead, we can use our own intense
experiences of hatred or depression to realize a deeper
truth about all of us living beings in general: none of us
are immune from this. Hell realm experiences present us
with an opportunity to extend care to ourselves by extending care to others. Taking the opportunity to regard even
those with whom we are angry with loving-kindness helps
us to begin to crawl out of the pit of despair. We can use our
own worst experiences to regain some perspective. Taking
advantage of such moments of clarity to express tenderness
toward our fellow travelers helps us rebuild our dignity and
sense of value, and the value of those around us.

When we use our own negative experiences to develop kindness and care for others, we truly transform the poisons of hatred and despair that afflict our hearts and minds into medicine that has the power to heal. As we cultivate an attitude of loving-kindness, we are also better able to see that, though they are dark and deep, the hell realms are also impermanent. Just a bit of goodwill toward those around us can go a long way to pulling us out.

THE PRACTICE:
LOVING-KINDNESS MEDITATION

In the hell realm, hatred and claustrophobia have seemingly eaten up all the space that might once have accommodated feelings of gentleness, appreciation, and kindness, both toward oneself and others. The single most powerful cause of being lost in a hell realm is the drying up of, or loss of access to, the wellspring of kindness that is a natural dimension of the human heart and experience.

When you are in a hell realm mindset, your experience is one of being lost in a barren desert without love, compassion, or sympathy. So when an opportunity arises, you can draw water in that desert from the well of loving-kindness. This aspect of ourselves remains in our hearts, buried under the rubble of misery. We can tap that underground spring using an ancient Buddhist practice called *maitri* in Sanskrit or *metta* in Pali. In English, it is simply called *loving-kindness* meditation.

The practice of cultivating loving-kindness is simple, direct, and effective. You extend loving-kindness to all beings, including those you love, those to whom you are indifferent, and even those you hate. Importantly, you also include yourself in this practice, which is challenging but fruitful if you find yourself feeling angry, unloved, and resentful, as is the case in the hell realm mindset. Loving-kindness is exactly what is missing in the hell realm, so this practice can be seen as a direct antidote to feeling stuck in a field of aggression and misery.

Naturally it's easier to generate positive wishes for people you love. For many of us this is our parents, our children, our pets, our teachers, or our friends. In these instances loving-kindness flows and we can connect with that energy to get the ball rolling. It is challenging to generate loving-kindness toward people to whom we are indifferent, and very challenging indeed to generate it toward people we don't like. Sometimes, as in the hell realms, it can be most challenging to extend loving-kindness to ourselves. With some patience and practice, you will find that the reach of your loving-kindness can be far and wide.

To prepare the ground for practicing loving-kindness, it is helpful to consider that the way in which we categorize other beings changes over time, sometimes even very quickly. Whatever we experience is subject to impermanence. For example, an anonymous person we once did not even know eventually became our friend or even life partner. Perhaps the marriage went sour, and we ended up parting as bitter enemies. Even one person can play all three roles of stranger, friend, and enemy in just one life. We can also recognize that the way we look at people is very much related to circumstances; our perceptions of others do not happen in a vacuum. If we are having a bad day, it is much easier to get irritated at somebody, maybe even somebody we fundamentally like. On a beautiful sunny spring day, everybody may look great, and we may more easily feel in love with everything and be happy. Causes and conditions set the stage for our attitudes toward the world, and we can (and do) affect those causes and conditions. It is practical to train our minds further so that we are not completely governed by our negative habitual patterns when we look at others.

Built on the foundation of these lines of thought, the loving-kindness meditation is fairly simple.

- Begin by taking a comfortable seat in a quiet place, bringing your attention to your breath, and settling into the present moment.
- Once your mind is settled, reflect briefly on imper-manence, particularly as it relates to the roles that others play in our lives: strangers, friends, and enemies.
- Close your eyes and think of somebody you love: a friend, relative, or lover. Open your heart to them and send them four positive wishes:
  - May you be safe.
  - May you be healthy.
  - May you be happy.
  - May you be at ease.

You can either repeat each wish a few times, imagining the person you wish it for, or you can just think about how those wishes might manifest and affect that person's life. Be creative about it!

- Next, repeat the wishes with respect to yourself. Then repeat this process successively with respect to a person you neither like nor dislike (somebody you don't know well or don't already have strong feelings about), and then with respect to someone you consider an enemy or antagonist (someone you do not like).
- Conclude the practice by radiating loving-kindness to all beings. Open your kind, sweet, loving heart to all beings, sending good wishes to all of them—friends, oneself, strangers, enemies, humans, animals, ghosts—anybody who comes to mind. Then simply dissolve the meditation and sit quietly for a moment or two.

As you practice, you may notice that your "enemy" changes over time, and that's fine. As mentioned already, yesterday's enemy can be tomorrow's ally. Also it's fine just to notice what comes up for you while you are trying to do this practice and simply allow space for that as well. Some may feel that the practice of loving-kindness is too touchy-feely. At first I thought maybe it was too innocent, too sweet. But it is an ancient practice dating all the way back to the Buddha and it is surprisingly powerful. It is a powerful antidote to the intense claustrophobia and aggression experienced in the hell realm. It is sometimes easier than practicing mindfulness/awareness meditation because it has direction and content. Sometimes in a hell realm state of mind it can be too painful to just sit and see what arises.

NINE

Karma and Freedom

KARMA CAN BE the engine of either imprisonment or liberation. Karma, as we have said, refers to the evolution of patterns of thought, emotions, and behavior. It is truly a neutral process. We have the potential to shape our karma through our intentions, and by becoming aware of the whole process we can shift the direction and momentum of our individual and collective karma. There is nothing fixed or predetermined about karma from that point of view. When we act out of craving, ignorance, or aggression, our karma intensifies and those motivations become negative patterns that shape our thoughts and actions. These patterns accumulate like barnacles and make us feel sluggish and blocked up. When our karma produces a mindset that feels especially thick and heavy, we have sunk into an experience of the three lower realms. This is what is meant by "bad karma."

When we act out of awareness and compassion, we tend

to develop positive karma that has a lighter, happier tone to it. The positive patterns created by these motivations produce circumstances beneficial to ourselves and others. On the basis of such good circumstances, we develop a mindset that inclines us to cultivate virtue, presence, and skillful action. When we have such mindsets we are experiencing the three higher realms. We have, by far, the greatest opportunity to develop such positive qualities in a human realm mindset, where the fluctuation between pleasure and pain leaves us too fixated neither on pain nor pleasure, but vulnerable and open to exploration and change. This is what is meant by "good karma."

Beyond sowing and reaping good and bad karma, a third possibility in the Wheel teachings is going beyond karma and attaining total freedom from the six realms altogether. In general when we practice these teachings, we are cultivating good karma by developing mindfulness and compassion and exploring the possibility of waking up completely from our daydream, whether it appears to be positive or negative. Ultimately the Wheel teachings point toward a state of natural wakefulness that transcends the notion of karma altogether.

In the original painting of the Wheel, the Buddha is depicted standing outside the wheel, not imprisoned or trapped by the forces of karma, as he has achieved liberation from these cycles. This is what the Buddha explicitly claimed to have accomplished. From that point onward a Buddha can actually choose to re-enter the realms in order to teach and assist others in their journey through them. Such beings are rare and precious, but they do manifest sometimes as powerfully realized individuals and teachers for the sake of the rest of us. That is why the original Wheel painting also portrays a Buddha within each of the six realms, teaching in a way that is accessible to the beings in those realms.

There are also teachers who have achieved some degree of freedom from the chains of karma but are still connected to the six realms and are still working with their own personal karma as well as that of others. These people are called *bodhisattvas*. They are our teachers and mentors and they themselves have made considerable progress in understanding the nature of samsaric existence and the problems and opportunities within the six realms. If we think about it, perhaps we have met somebody like that already.

KARMA AND BILLIARDS

When we take a deep look at who we are, we still see some kind of continuity to our ever-changing existence, even though we may not actually find an independent and permanent entity called *me*. Exploring that continuity is how we can come to understand the notion of karma.

Karma literally means "action," particularly as it relates to the continuity of cause and effect. In a way it's like shooting pool. If we're dazed and confused as we play the game, then we're just sort of knocking the balls all over the place. If there's clarity and precision as you set up your shot, the balls go where you want them to go. When we look at our pool table, we can see the balls form a pattern, just as in this very moment the various elements of our lives form some kind of pattern. As we survey our situation on the table, we have some kind of response to it, and we prepare to take our next shot. As we pick up our pool cue, we have some assessment, some feeling, and some kind of intention going forward.

When we take our shot, we not only move the cue ball (me), but we also affect the motion and pattern of all the other balls (others) on the table. In so doing we create a new situation, albeit one that is highly dependent on the immediately previous situation. We can't just take all the balls off the table and place them wherever we want in the middle of a game (life). So every moment has its own unique patterning as we approach it. Based on our past thoughts and actions, mixed with our current intentions, we move ourselves through life and move those around us. If we can learn to see the patterns of our actions and their effects, over time we will develop an understanding of how the karma game of our lives works.

Positive karma—again, a relative term—basically describe a series of actions in which our intention and efforts move our lives in a positive direction, that is, a pattern of action that moves both ourselves and others toward some kind of desirable outcome. We can think of such good outcomes as similar to a good lay of billiard balls on the table: it leaves us with a clear view of a reasonable sequence of mostly accessible shots. For example you might end up in a good situation, living a relatively wakeful life in a sympathetic environment, actually able to enjoy yourself and appreciate your existence, and foster positive circumstances for yourself and the people around you.

Negative karma basically describes those situations in which our intentions and efforts have left us with a counterproductive arrangement of circumstances. This would correspond to a bad lay of the balls on the table, with lots of tough angles and no reasonable sequence for progressing through the table. We might find ourselves in a difficult situation, in response to which we have become angry and resentful, and therefore find ourselves in an unpleasant and challenging environment day after day.

SEEING OUR OWN KARMA

If we are going to take the time to practice meditation, study teachings like the Wheel, and especially if we are going to make any attempt to present these teachings and practices to others, we ourselves must engage in a process of self-scrutiny and be ready to reveal the truth about ourselves to ourselves. There is no external confirmation that will enable us to transcend the need for this kind of examination.

Underlying the process of self-examination is the assumption that we are fundamentally whole and good human beings from the very beginning. Therefore, we can afford to look into ourselves deeply, with compassion. Without gentleness and kindness, when we move toward self-scrutiny and honest exploration, we might burn out fairly quickly. When many people try to meditate, they realize that it is not a magic tranquility pill, and that simply do not have enough compassion for themselves to undertake what is actually an in-depth exploration of their whole being, warts and all. The intolerance we express toward others is often a product of the intolerance we already feel toward ourselves. Sometimes we may find that it is even easier to be tolerant and kind to others than to ourselves.

It will be very challenging indeed to progress along any kind of path of awakening or discovery without a good healthy dose of loving-kindness in our supply kit. Without loving-kindness, our path is going to be exceedingly steep and narrow.

THREE POISONOUS ATTITUDES

Right at the very center of the traditional Wheel of Life are three animals that represent passion (rooster), aggression (snake), and ignorance (pig). They each have the tail of the animal in front of them in their mouth—creating a loop with endless momentum. If we think of these three as active verbs—grasping, aggressing, and ignoring—rather than nouns, it helps to illustrate that these three actively create our core attitude or mood. These three processes are the heart of our programmed responses to situations and are the roots of all our karma. On the basis of these fundamental responses we develop all kinds of sophisticated, multi-tiered narratives that become the fabric of our lives in the six realms.

GRASPING

Sometimes we grasp at ideas, people, places, things, and emotions in order to stabilize a sense of our own existence: who we are, what our world is like, and who belongs in here with us. Grasping is more than the simple experience of being attracted to something or someone. It is an attempt to control the things or people that we crave in a way that helps us define ourselves and our territory. We use grasping to create a solid distinction between our world and the bigger world, based on identifying and solidifying what is ours. Of course attraction is a natural process, as is attempting to draw in those things to which we are attracted.

When we see a beautiful blue jay or the redness of an apple, we naturally want to take those things from the greater world and have them become part of our personal world. When we fall in love, we move that person from the cast of thousands into a very special cast of two. We actually might feel that that person is now ours alone, our special domain; if somebody else admires them, we might feel jealousy and pain. Most importantly, we take a naturally flowing event, such as attraction, and solidify it to create territory: this object is now "mine" and will reinforce my sense of "me" existing in a solid way.

By grasping so tightly—one could even say desperately—at the objects of our attraction, we create a situation that is difficult, tense, and eventually painful. The flip side of grasping is the pain of having to let go: when our lover leaves us for another, when our kids go off to college, or when beauty, youth, and health abandon us.

AGGRESSING

Alternatively sometimes we will exclude, eliminate, or push away those elements that we do not want to include in our world. Aggressing can give us a very solid sense of clear boundaries, defining our territory and that which is outside of it. Some people would say that aggressing has the strongest negative karmic consequences. When we look at our mind in meditation, many of us find that aggressive feelings dig in deep and hard. It is not so easy to let them go.

There is often some kind of hurt or wound underlying our aggression. When we contemplate our own aggressive feelings, there is often a feeling of having been disregarded, unappreciated, even attacked mentally or emotionally or physically. There are very powerful emotional and physiological trigger points for anger. We may have been in a situation in which our safety and well-being were legitimately threatened, and we found ourselves in a fight-or-flight mode. An aggressive response to a dangerous situation can get wired into our psyche and body chemistry and become a powerful habitual response whenever we feel threatened by real or imaginary circumstances.

As a strategy, aggressing can effectively help us to maintain our solid sense of self. In grasping we might want to merge with the other, so sometimes the boundary between ourselves and somebody else will not be so clear. In aggressing the lines are clearly drawn. This territory is mine and I will define it further by excluding you from it.

Aggressing is perhaps the strongest basis for solidifying our existence in the realms, as is evidenced by its starring role in the hell realm experience. The experience of concentrated, endless aggression characterizes the most intense, painful, and claustrophobic diorama of all—the hell realm. Here, we are trapped with the unrelenting experience of not wanting to be where we are, which is perhaps the simplest definition of suffering.

IGNORING

Ignoring is, in a way, the most insidious kind of strategy to define our territory. When we ignore in this way we are sidelining or generally not acknowledging those aspects of our reality that we neither want to include by grasping, nor to explicitly exclude by aggressing. Rather than actively trying to include or exclude, we simply relegate a large part of our experience to the realm of other by simply not noticing it.

Ignoring can be the most comprehensive and efficient tactic for creating a sense of territory. If grasping is shining a spotlight on what we desire and aggressing is roasting undesirables under a heat lamp, then ignoring is like turning off the lights with one flick of the switch. That which does not fit into our solid sense of self is comprehensively and inclusively cordoned off, into oblivion.

When we talk about ignorance as ignoring, we can see that it is a process, a choice, an operating mode. Ignoring can be powerfully effective at creating a space in which we are completely insulated and secure from any kind of input or feedback we find troublesome. In certain situations ignoring can be much more effective than grasping or aggressing at creating and defending our territory.

The quality of ignoring is most prominent in the god and animal realms. There is a kind of numbness, turning off any stimuli that break the self-absorbed cocoon of these environments. We could say that the animal realm is a dull kind of ignoring and the god realm is a brilliant kind of ignoring, but what they have in common is a powerful inertia, a deep desire to keep things as they are. The recognition of impermanence is masked, and anything that interrupts our predictable environment is excluded.

Though most prominent in those two realms, however, it should be clear that ignoring is actually our most fundamental tactic and underlies all of the realms. What is really being ignored is the sharp edge of our natural awareness.

VIRTUOUS AND NONVIRTUOUS ACTIONS

We see positive and negative karma depicted in a ring that circles the three poisons at the hub of the wheel. In the traditional image we see devils dragging helplessly bound victims down to hell on the right side of the ring, and virtuous scouts climbing their way to the heavenly realms on the left side. These images represent those virtuous and nonvirtuous actions that keep the wheel spinning. Traditionally these actions are broken down into lists of ten:

TEN NONVIRTUOUS ACTIONS	TEN VIRTUOUS ACTIONS
1. Taking a life	1. Not killing
2. Taking what is not given	2. Not stealing
3. Sexual misconduct (causing harm through inappropriate sexual activity)	3. Avoiding sexual misconduct
4. Deceit	4. Not deceiving
5. Slander of others	5. Avoiding slander of others
6. Uttering harsh words	6. Avoiding harsh words
7. Empty speech	7. Avoiding empty speech

8. Greed	8. Not being greedy
9. Malice	9. Not being malicious
10. Holding wrong views (such as nihilism and eternalism)	10. Avoiding wrong views

As we can see, the virtuous actions are mostly framed as avoiding the nonvirtuous ones. This is because a large part of developing virtue is refraining from actions that cause harm to ourselves and others. In Sanksrit refraining from harm in this way is called *ahimsa*, an important concept in most yoga schools. Trungpa Rinpoche used to call this aspect of our discipline the "Big No." It is self-explanatory, but sometimes bears repeating and contemplation.

Recognizing the residual consequences of our actions can make us much more sensitive to the power and impact of how we manage our states of mind and our behavior. Everybody knows that if, when we get into a disagreement with someone close to us, we become aggravated and hostile, there will be consequences later on. Most harmful actions leave some kind of trail or imprint on our own internal environment (troubling thoughts and emotions), our body (stress, injury, and sickness), our relationship to others (unresolved feelings), and our physical environment (pollution). It is not a big stretch to understand that actions taken with a fundamentally positive attitude will ripple on in a certain way, and actions taken on the basis of passion, aggression, and ignorance will ripple on in a different way.

If we act with full awareness, if we are truly awake, we will stop creating karma. The ripple of unconscious behavior will actually cease. But somewhere between here and there, between our daydream world and being fully awake, we do regularly have access to behaving in a relatively more "enlightened" way. By not sowing negative seeds through negative actions, we can actually create a more hospitable environment for ourselves and everyone around us.

The teachings are not particularly advocating repression of our negative habits, but rather changing our allegiance to favor healthier and more productive attitudes and actions. The first step is to see clearly where we are, without trying to ignore our patterns or force change. Then we can gradually redirect our thoughts and behavior toward more beneficial outlooks and outcomes. That is the implication of studying this ring of the wheel and contemplating our positive and negative actions in everyday life.

THE CHAIN OF KARMIC ACTION

The outermost ring of the wheel depicts the chain of dependently arising actions that produce existence in any given realm of the wheel. This cycle describes how, on the basis of fundamental ignorance, we are propelled into birth, old age, sickness, and death, over and over again. It is yet another way of describing how our karma evolves. In the classical diagram, the links are symbolized as follows:

THE TWELVE LINKS OF DEPENDENT ARISING
1. Ignorance (a blind man feeling his way with a cane)
2. Mental Formations (a potter making pots)

3. Consciousness (a monkey leaping from branch to branch in a tree)
4. Name and Form (two people in a boat)
5. Six Sense Gates (a building with six apertures)
6. Contact (a couple kissing)
7. Sensation (a man with an arrow in his eye)
8. Craving, desire, or thirst (a person drinking alcohol)
9. Attachment (a person reaching out to grasp a fruit on a branch)
10. Becoming (a couple in sexual embrace)
11. Birth (a baby being born)
12. Old age, sickness, and death (a coffin waiting for burial)

From that first moment of ignorance, a succession of experiences arise, each of which is dependent on the previous one. The causes represent a breakdown of how chains of karma are formed, almost like time-lapse photography. The message is that if we do not break this chain of causation, we will continue to cycle through samsaric existence, moving endlessly through the six realms, moment to moment, year to year, and lifetime to lifetime. Something has to break this cycle to wake us up from these repetitive patterns.

We could say that each moment of this cycle is meaningful, but two in particular have perhaps greater significance. The first is the original moment of ignorance, or of ignoring, when we lose our awareness. It is at that moment that we begin to fall into our daydream and lose the sharp, clear edge of our natural wakefulness.

The second moment is the space between craving and attachment. It is exactly between craving and attachment, or grasping, that karma is solidified. Think about the moment at 10 p.m. on Thursday evening between craving ice cream and the moment at 10:01 p.m. when we mysteriously find ourselves with the refrigerator door open and the ice cream, bowl, and scooper in hand. Think about the moment in an argument when we feel that we are losing our temper, before we raise our voices. Those tiny cracks between craving and acting on craving, or aggravation and acting on aggravation, are where the formation of karma is either solidified or interrupted.

Many meditation techniques consist of drawing our attention to this moment or gap and then holding it there. Instead of taking that next step and taking action, we simply see that craving come and let it go, firmly planted on our cushion. With awareness, we can see our negative patterns arise, ripen, and then just allow them to exist as mental events without further acting on them. This practice breaks the chain reaction of karma, moment to moment.

KARMA AND INTENTIONS

Negative actions—lying, cheating, stealing, killing, and so on—caused by negative emotions—such as passion, aggression, and ignorance—cause negative outcomes that create harm for oneself and others. The actions that we do are purely relative on their own. An action that might cause harm in one situation can be a lifesaver in a different one. For example a robber might use a knife to cut his victim, causing deep wounds, fear, trauma, and pain. A surgeon might take another knife and cut deep into her patient, removing a life-threatening blood clot or cancer. We might, in the spirit of generosity, give a beggar money hoping to help him feed his family, but he might drink himself to death with the booze he buys with that money.

It is not always so easy to clearly see all the implications of even our simplest acts. If we clarify our intention, at least we have a sense of trying to create a positive outcome. If we do nothing to refine our thoughts and actions, we will no doubt continue to act primarily from deeply ingrained habits and become further entrenched in behaviors based on grasping, aggressing, and ignoring.

We can create bad karma with the best of intentions and good karma with the worst. However, when we combine seeing clearly with a positive motivation, we are in the best position to avoid creating further negative karma.

Good karma comes from cultivating patterns of benevolent thoughts and actions that create positive circumstances for ourselves and others. Positive actions—helping, teaching, caring, and so on—born of positive qualities—such as generosity, patience, and discernment—create positive outcomes that benefit ourselves and others. If, for example, we have the intention to be genuinely helpful to others and we can see clearly what is needed in a given situation, we are able to provide care and meaningful feedback to those around us.

USING SKILLFUL MEANS

Two things are crucial to the development of positive karma: discernment—clearly seeing the lay of the land in any given situation—and skillful means—knowing what action will be truly effective. Traditionally when we talk about using skillful means to create good karma, we are referring to four strategies that help shape a positive intention into a skillful action: pacifying aggressive situations, enriching impoverished situations, magnetizing isolated situations, and destroying harmful situations.

Pacifying aggressive situations means to approach even intensely disruptive or violent situations with a spacious and peaceful attitude, free from stress and panic. We look calmly at all the elements of a potentially volatile situation and bring perspective and the kind of spaciousness that allows others to dial down their emotions. A savvy police officer does this when skillfully breaking up a family dispute or a confrontation on the street. We bring equilibrium to the situation, and because we have perspective we can talk somebody off the ledge of emotional upheaval.

Enriching impoverished situations means to approach even adverse situations with a sense of resourcefulness and cheer. We adopt an attitude that helps others to experience the richness and positive potential of their world and their role in it. Our actions create opportunity and a sense of fulfillment in place of a sense of alienation and poverty. The people who volunteer and run afterschool sports programs for troubled teenagers show us examples of this type of skillful behavior.

Magnetizing isolated situations means to work with someone who feels lonely and cut off to help them feel included and welcome. By adopting a naturally confident and uplifted attitude ourselves, we become a beacon for others. They are drawn to us and become curious about our perspective and choices. Many great teachers have this quality and are known to quite naturally help their students flourish. This quality is similar to charisma. Sometimes we call it "authentic presence."

Destroying harmful situations means to cut through negativity and eliminate strong patterns that obstruct well-being and growth. We say no to confusion, aggression, and dangerous situations with clarity and directness. Taking a knife away from a small child who is not ready to handle it is a modest example of this action. Taking a knife away from a belligerent adult is perhaps a more poignant example. We can first try talking them down (pacifying an aggressive situation), then making them feel better (enriching an impoverished situation), and then we can empathize with them (magnetizing an isolated situation). If none of that works, we may have to disarm the person directly. In the world of karma, we can sometimes face challenging situations that may not conform to our ideal, spiritual universe.

Creating positive karma is not always a walk in the park. We have to work with real-life situations as they arise, and have to be able to think skillfully according to what the situation calls for. We cannot just wish ourselves into a peaceful place based on ignoring all the passion and aggression in our world. That would perhaps be more like the limited approach of the god realm, right?

BEYOND KARMA

Transcending karma altogether comes with being continuously present and aware. When we have achieved this type of total peace, there is no longer any grasping, aggressing, or ignoring, and consequently no karmic seeds being planted or grown, and no daydream of the six realms. Transcending karma altogether by continuous presence is radical. Most of our activity in this world, even including most forms of spiritual practice, is based on positioning the self in relation to perceived opportunities, threats, and whatever else is going on. To simply rest in present awareness, without the self-based agenda, is practically unheard of and definitely not taught in the schools I attended.

In fact quite often it is thought that if we focused on the present in this way, we would be dysfunctional. This is incorrect. Great masters like Trungpa Rinpoche, Dilgo Khyentse Rinpoche, and His Holiness the Sixteenth Karmapa, whom I have had the privilege of seeing in action, are each able to manifest in such diverse ways that I had to wonder at times if there was only one person in there. They somehow embody a balance of complete stillness and cutting-edge activity. Their actions feel utterly strategic and completely spontaneous at the same time.

However, if we don't see some modeling of the awakened state of mind, it can be very difficult to even imagine it as a possibility. The link, forged largely through our own practice, is that we can begin to recognize an awakened quality in ourselves that is free from the thick webbing of our past and anxious anticipation of our future. There is a kind of fundamental freedom that we can experience—even if only for a moment—in this very moment.

According to the Wheel teachings, this awakened mind, free of both positive and negative karmic patterns, is our true legacy and our most treasured possession. We already have it by nature and if we choose to do so, can activate it completely within this very lifetime. If we choose that road, the Wheel and the six realms become a roadmap of liberation and a path toward freedom. We are being given a map of the prison in which we are currently confined. That is why the King of Magadha, after he was given the original painting of the Wheel and contemplated its meaning, was said to have achieved liberation from the six realms. Of course as soon as we conceptualize this kind of freedom, fixate on it and try to hold onto it, we are creating causes and conditions for cycling through the six realms once again.

Some teachers these days claim to have achieved this kind of freedom, but just like the Buddha in his day, their claim must be challenged and manifested in every situation to be verifiable. My own personal experience is that studying and understanding the Wheel and finding freedom from the myriad forms of entrapment portrayed therein is a long and winding road. Just try to stop eating sweets for a month, for example, and you will see how hard that is. Can you even imagine how hard it is to be totally liberated from the myriad forms of grasping, aggressing, and ignoring, altogether?

TEN

Grandmother's Advice for Practice

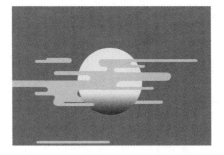

WHAT TO EXPECT ALONG THE WAY

Particularly when getting started with meditation, we can expect to have our minds be active, full of the habitual activity of the six realms, and somewhat resistant to the idea of awakening from the daydream. We can expect irritation, boredom, neurotic upheavals, physical discomfort, and doubt as to whether this all makes sense in the first place. That is a healthy beginning!

In the Tibetan tradition there is something called "grandmother's advice": just simple, practical, earthy words from a little old lady who's been there.

Somehow the more expectation and ambition we have with our meditation practice, the more disappointment and irritation we are likely to experience. Some of the least helpful instructions we can ever give a new meditator is "just quiet your mind and relax." So many people are hopeful that meditation will bring them tranquility and ease and peace and joy. What about our pain, our confusion, our turbulence? Where are we going to put all those things? Do we just sweep them under the rug and hope they'll go away while we create our little bubble of peace and bliss?

So for starters, it is good to help manage people's expectations. Meditation can include boredom, irritation, discomfort, frustration, grasping, aggression, a discursive waterfall of thoughts and emotions coming and going, and perhaps occasionally a sense of peace and acceptance of things as they are. It can also include insight, awareness, stability, and delight. In a nutshell, it can and will include all the aspects of who we are and of what our lives are actually made.

Along the way, though, if we practice diligently, we are likely to develop insight as to how our minds work and how we get lost in the six realms. It is a gradual process. Patience and effort will ultimately be more valuable than ambition.

TAKING A FRIENDLY ATTITUDE

It is best to take a gentle, friendly attitude toward ourselves right from the beginning. Compassion will do a lot to assuage the grasping, aggressing, and ignoring that persists even when practicing meditation. The single most powerful ally we have as we explore and awaken from our daydream is gentleness and kindness toward ourselves. How many of us can say that we have learned how to be truly kind and gentle with ourselves? We've heard about it, we've talked about it, we've espoused it perhaps, but how many of us have actually done it? Learning to be kind toward ourselves is possible, but it takes intention and patience. It is not a habit for most of us and it is not the orientation of life in the six realms. Gentleness and compassion have little to do with having things conform to our agenda or timetable.

Perhaps a majority of the meditation students come to the practice with a strong project mentality. It's as if once they get this meditation thing under their belt, they can finally have some peace of mind and be even more efficient and together. Needless to say, in such situations there is often a kind of frustration, impatience, and even early burnout, as they begin to realize that there is no magic bullet. The practice is slow and steady and requires diligence and patience. The two things missing from such an approach are gentleness and curiosity. We should take the same approach as we would when caring for a child. Helping a child can bring out the tenderness in us. It's a good model for working with others and it's an especially good model for working with ourselves.

EXERTION

There will be many times when we don't want to practice, don't want to study, don't want to go any further, and we just want to wrap ourselves back up in the sleepy cocoon of the six realms. We are strongly acclimated to the realms and it will take effort to overcome that inertia.

If we meditate and work with the elements of our lives as a spiritual journey, we may not be running and re-running our established programs, but we are still swimming upstream. This takes quite a lot of effort and energy. We will have to overcome the inertia of our life in the six realms, which will require a strong point of view, some kind of faith that there is another possibility, and fearless, relentless effort.

Practicing meditation is not really that different from any other kind of practice. We will almost assuredly reach a point—later, or often sooner—where we feel that we have lost interest, or motivation, and have even forgotten why we started in the first place. We will experience boredom, irritation, and frustration: all kinds of seductive thoughts that will pull us away from our practice.

The key then is to remember what we are doing, why we are doing it, and to lean into our resistance. Sometimes just getting to the cushion is the antidote. All of us will face these moments in our training, so Grandma thought it might be helpful to mention it here.

PATIENCE

Patience is how we quiet our own aggression. This is a very particular, dynamic kind of patience, though. It is not the kind where we grit our teeth and suffer through difficult situations. Nor is it like the ignoring of the animal and god realms, where we put important things out of mind. Rather, this dynamic patience is a wakeful presence, where we release some of our expectation and ambition regarding what happens next, allowing us to ride the changing tide of any situation. If we rigidly adhere to our own expectations and ambitions, situations appear as strong obstacles. If on the other hand we are strongly committed to our practice and this open presence, those same obstacles can be transformed into opportunities to deepen our practice.

For this reason, our practice is an ideal place to learn patience. In meditation we are better off letting go of our ambitions, concerning ourselves less with results than with process. This sentiment is sometimes expressed through such sayings as "abandon all hope of fruition" and "path without goal." At some point we are no longer practicing from a goal-oriented point of view. We are just expressing ourselves.

It may take a lot of time to let go of our expectations and ambitions, even with diligent practice, but the good news is that patience is a self-cultivating virtue. If we wait long enough to attain it, we will have it.

QUIETING THE MIND

Many students come to meditation practice with this objective. They have noticed their chaotic, monkey-like mind and would like some kind of relief, like taking an aspirin for a headache. I think that meditation does, in a sense, ultimately provide some kind of relief, not by suppressing our monkey mind but, initially at least, by making friends with the monkey. The warfare between the monkey and our desire for peace and quiet can be a powerful conflict in our practice, especially in the beginning.

Many students sit for five minutes and say they just can't take even one more minute because their mind is so restless that it is driving them crazy. It's like they're being taken on a roller coaster tour of the six realms. The restlessness they experience is in direct contrast to the peaceful mood they hope the meditation practice will bring. They hope they can bypass the pattern of their very active thoughts, and just abruptly have their mind be quiet and still. From that point of view, it seems that many of us are actually looking for meditation to function as a tranquilizer.

There are certain techniques like mindfulness that can quiet our minds down in a sense, but that is not really the point. A much more potent approach is to take the attitude that whatever arises in our mind is manageable and we do not have to try to conquer it with an aggressive and goal-oriented approach.

Suzuki Roshi used to say that the best way to calm your cow or horse down is to give it a large spacious meadow in which to wander. Then it will calm down on its own. For some of us, we want to put a bridle on the horse and a bit in its mouth, and try to forcefully quiet it down. This approach is rarely successful and usually creates further stress and anxiety as we try to control the horse in our mind as it travels through the realms. Perhaps then we get frustrated and abandon the whole project altogether.

With meditation practice, some degree of balance and tranquility is definitely a goal, but it is only a step in the process of developing a more profound level of openness, and insight as to the nature of our situation.

If we examine the instructions for mindfulness, we will notice that nowhere in the technique does it ever say "now quiet your mind." That is actually not a particularly effective meditation instruction. The instructions are much more precise and more doable. The instruction tells us to place our attention on our breathing and the feeling of the present moment, and when we notice that it is elsewhere simply bring it back. We cultivate present awareness by coming back to the awareness of the breath and to the moment. There is never any mention of extinguishing thought. This is a subtle but extremely important point. We are being given a task that is achievable. When you notice your awareness is in the daydream, simply bring it back to the present. If we said suppress or eliminate the daydream mind to which we are so habituated, almost nobody would be able to do it and eventually we would have a full-scale exodus from the meditation hall.

KEEPING THE EYES OPEN

What is being cultivated in mindfulness meditation practice is a quality of attentiveness that will bring us out of our six-realm daydream world and into a clear and open relationship with the world around us. From that point of view, meditation is not seen as an escape from reality. Rather, it is a method to fully engage present reality. Therefore, we can meditate with our eyes open with a soft downward gaze. With our eyes closed there is a tendency to turn inward, zone out, even sleep. With our eyes gently open, there is less of a dramatic split between the internal and external worlds. We are more porous and our awareness can still engage reality.

If, on the other hand, our eyes are wide open, we can focus too much energy in the visual field and be distracted by that. By lowering our gaze, especially when we are getting started, we do contain our visual field and sense perceptions in general. We are allowing the space and time to have a closer look at how our state of mind comes in and out of being, and we are taming the wilder quality of our mind that jumps around from realm to realm like a crazed monkey.

When we get up from our seat and extend our meditation practice into other activities—such as walking, eating, work, or relationship—we will need to have our eyes open. If we cannot eventually sustain the quality of presence in our everyday life, our meditation will just become a specialized activity, a way to generate a temporary feeling of peace and ease that will not stand up to the challenges of everyday life. If we practice with our eyes slightly open, it will be easier for us to keep our focus when we are doing things in daily life. That is the logic for keeping the gaze open, but also somewhat subdued, and slightly downward.

WHEN STRONG EMOTIONS ARISE

Sometimes during our practice and in everyday life, we may experience a surge of strong emotions. We might experience this as a physical sensation, like feeling the tightening of our muscles when we get angry, or an aching in our heart when we feel loss or longing; or we might experience it as even more atmospheric and abstract. Many people have asked: "What do I do with these powerful feelings? Do I label my emotions 'thinking' and just bypass them in order to bring my attention back to my breath?"

We can take a middle path between repressing and indulging these powerful feelings. If we examine emotions, they appear to be a made up of a particular storyline combined with a more energetic quality. From that point of view the emotions, even though they may make us feel claustrophobic and can be difficult to process, are actually a key to our core energy and life force as human beings. Through meditation practice, we are not attempting to suppress and eliminate our emotions; that would turn us into some kind of meditation zombie. Sometimes we might feel like that, or see other people who look like that, but that is not really what we are hoping to achieve, right?

When we practice, if we can get in touch with the feeling of our emotions without attaching to them, trying to avoid or manipulate them, we are actually experiencing the full force of being alive and present in that moment. In the Buddhist view the cloudy and troubling quality of feelings can be transformed into a clear sensation in which the emotions are seen to contain the qualities of aliveness, vividness, and dynamic communication.

Obviously, for most of us, that is a huge step. The approach that we can take right away is to allow our emotions to arise, recognize them as fundamentally workable, and also to see that they are impermanent, that we are not stuck with them or doomed by them in any fundamental way.

ELEVEN

The Importance of Mentors and Friends along the Way

DIFFERENT KINDS OF TEACHERS

As we explore our relationship to the Wheel through meditation, it is extremely helpful to get some individual direction and feedback from a teacher. Of course there are different kinds of teachers, different levels of capability, ranging from beginner to intermediate to advanced, just like students. Recognizing which is which is important. There is a Buddha depicted in each realm in the wheel, representing skillful engagement with the energy of that realm. There is also a Buddha depicted outside of the wheel, representing the possibility of awakening from the daydream world altogether. A teacher is always available.

In traditional Buddhism there are three levels of teachers, ranging from preceptor/elder to mentor/spiritual friend, to master/guru. The preceptor/elder is kind of like a high-school teacher. They have definitely studied the subject and know more about it than we do. They are passing along certain accumulated knowledge from their particular discipline, designing a course of study for their students, administering tests, and perhaps offering some feedback. However, they are not necessarily giving any kind of personal counseling, life lessons, or modeling a code of behavior for us.

The mentor/spiritual friend has definitely progressed further along the spiritual path than we have. They may not be fully realized themselves, but they have some deep insight into their subject and personal experience. They are available to us for personal counseling and have an interest in our life and our well-being. In a sense they accompany us on our journey through the six realms and serve as colleague and advisor.

The master teacher/guru is a very advanced level of teacher. The master teacher must be thoroughly knowledgeable and accomplished in the subject. In Buddhism the master or guru teaches us how to work with life in many dimensions. Sometimes the guru-disciple relationship is compared with a phase in martial art training where the master introduces real weapons. The meditation teacher is properly introducing us to reality. Such a teacher is deeply experienced with the six realms and knows all the traps and possibilities. We find that we are working beyond theory with our actual lives. The teacher at this level has a seamless and at times seemingly magical relationship with reality and handles the world masterfully.

My teacher, Trungpa Rinpoche, gave life lessons to his students on every conceivable level. This kind of relationship is truly unique and rare. It cannot be faked or approximated. In the Buddhist tradition there are serious safeguards and criteria for somebody putting out their shingle as a master, but of course there is no guarantee. Therefore we have to ultimately rely on our own counsel as to the genuineness of a teacher and the appropriateness of studying with him or her.

I have found that presenting these guidelines regarding the three levels of teachers has been very helpful for students as they go deeper into their practice of meditation. Certainly, for beginners, they are often in need of a preceptor who can give good instruction and foundation and perhaps later on some quality mentoring. Obviously a master teacher can function as a preceptor or mentor as well. That is a very fortunate situation when it occurs.

HOW TO FIND A TEACHER

So many students these days, at workshops and lectures, have asked, "How do I find a teacher?" In the classical Buddhist teachings there are all kinds of credentials and trainings, levels of accomplishment, and recognition. My teacher's teacher spent fifteen years alone in a cave meditating. How many of us would accept that criterion for our teacher training certificate? While we might be awed by this kind of credential, it may not speak to what we want from our own practice. Therefore there is a great need for good teachers who understand the perspective of those of us living in the very modern, industrialized world. There are also meditative traditions that incorporate our day-to-day life as an important element of the practice. Remember, the Wheel itself was given to a king, not a monk.

So, when we are looking for a teacher to help us with our budding meditation practice, I believe the first thing we should do is actually look. Looking can include reading, attending lectures, online exploration, workshops and retreats, asking questions, arranging a personal interview, and so on. It is a good sign if you feel connected and inspired, and if the surroundings, other students, and general atmosphere are appropriate and workable for you.

The general recommendation is that once we have done our due diligence, really investigated properly and settled on a particular teacher, hopefully with some kind of verifiable training themselves, we will dig in a bit and stay with the teaching even if obstacles arise.

In the beginning our fickleness can serve us, manifesting as diligent exploration of alternatives. In the middle our fickleness can take the form of jumping ship and catching another ride that might appear momentarily more glamorous, and this might well be counterproductive for us. All along the way we might discover other viable alternatives, and being aware of other approaches and their methods can make us a well-rounded and open-minded individual. Still, we must remember that our goal is not really to become a jack-of-all-trades and master of none.

Finally, there are many qualified meditation teachers in the West. There are many great books in our own language and cultural framework, and tremendous opportunities to study and practice within a variety of bona fide traditions. When I went to Bhutan, it was relatively difficult to see certain teachers, some of whom also teach in the West, often in very accessible contexts. There are also Western teachers who have studied and practiced diligently for many years and are wonderful teachers with a strong grasp on the mindset and needs of Western students.

LINEAGE AND TRADITION

A pedigree and a clear indication of thorough training can be a very positive element, but it is not a guarantee. Authenticity is clearly more important than credentials, but if someone is masking or hiding their background, not forthcoming about with whom, how, and when they studied and practiced, is not clear about their own lineage, that might not be a good thing.

In the Buddhist tradition there are many kinds of lineages or schools of training and practice. Some go back hundreds and hundreds of years and all of them, in some sense, go back 2,500 years to the actual teachings of the Buddha. A lineage is really a container for the accumulated experience and wisdom of a group of individuals over time, perhaps covering a variety of locations, even different nations. Remember, the Wheel of Life teachings presented in this book date all the way back to the time of the Buddha and have been passed along intact to us through a long line of dedicated and thoughtful practitioners and through several cultural extrapolations.

TRUSTING OUR OWN MINDS

When all is said and done, we ourselves are the final judge and jury of which teacher to study with and when to walk on by. I think for most of us, if we are interested in learning about meditation, we may not need a guru at all in the beginning stages of our practice. It would be great to find a solid preceptor who has actually studied, actually practiced, and can present the teachings to us in a clear and accessible way. That alone is rare enough. Later on we might truly benefit from the second-stage teacher, a spiritual friend, who can "mentor" us and give us some personal guidance and feedback on our journey. Such a teacher will quite possibly be highly aware of their own capability and their own shortcomings. They should be an experienced practitioner and show some of the qualities you are hoping to develop, but no doubt they will be human and still making their own progress, in any case. However we go about choosing a teacher, we need to feel comfortable and confident that we have looked around, and that, for this leg of our journey, we trust this person to work with us in these ways. That trust must be earned and verified by our experience.

If at some point we are studying with a master, the same criteria still apply. The teacher and their community should be modeling the qualities we aspire to manifest to some extent. But in the deeper practice, as mentioned above, we often find ourselves acutely aware of how stuck in the six realms we actually are. In this case, the teacher might be better compared to a surgeon. We may need some powerful insight to help cut through our patterned behaviors that we seem to cycle through over and over again. If we are choosing a surgeon, we should choose wisely, check out their training and their track record, and go into the relationship with some confidence and trust.

TRANSFORMING CONFUSION INTO WISDOM

Our confusion, anxiety, and discomfort are a significant part of the ground and fuel for our journey. We cannot simply repress them or throw them out and then hope that wisdom will remain. We actually have to find the wisdom within our confusion. It is a process of transformation.

A valuable piece of wisdom for us to recognize is that the life we currently have is fundamentally good and will be the basis for any enlightened existence to which we aspire. I think that many of us feel if we could only get rid of our stuff, our junk, even ourselves, that then we could experience a brighter day, a better world, sometime off in the future. Once we understand the Wheel and assess where we are in it, the basic message is that whatever situation we currently are in is workable and that the possibility of transforming our particular style of pain and confusion is always present.

The Wheel is a portrait of samsara, but it is also a portrait of the potential transformation of our life circumstances from pain and confusion into wisdom and compassion. These teachings are not intended to merely mirror our lives in an unflattering way and leave us stranded. They are a key to recognizing and changing our lives—they encourage and guide us as we awaken from our daydream.

The Wheel of Life: Illusion's Game

CHÖGYAM TRUNGPA RINPOCHE

THE WHOLE DHARMA is the language of samsara. That is why this painting is called the wheel of life, or *bhavachakra*, the wheel of existence, or becoming (samsara). This wheel is the portrait of samsara and therefore also of nirvana, which is the undoing of the samsaric coil. This image provides a good background for understanding illusion's game, based as it is on the four noble truths as the accurate teaching of being in the world. The outer ring of the nidanas describes the truth of suffering; the inner ring of the six realms describes the impetus of suffering; and the center of the wheel describes the origin of suffering, which is the path.

The wheel of life is always shown as being held by Yama (a personification meaning death, or that which provides the space for birth, death, and survival). Yama is the environment, the time for birth and death. In this case, it is the compulsive nowness in which the universe recurs. It provides the basic medium in which the different stages of the nidanas can be born and die.

The outer ring of the evolutionary stages of suffering is the twelve nidanas. *Nidana* means "chain," or chain reaction. The nidanas are that which presents the chance to evolve to a crescendo of ignorance or death. The ring of nidanas may be seen in terms of causality or accident from one situation to the next; inescapable coincidence brings a sense of imprisonment and pain, for you have been processed through this gigantic factory as raw material. You do not usually look forward to the outcome, but on the other hand, there is no alternative.

The death of the previous nidana gives birth to the next one within the realm of time, which is itself compulsive. Rather than one ending and another beginning, each nidana contains the quality of the previous one. Within this realm of possibility, the twelve nidanas develop.

The first stage is ignorance, *avidya*. This is represented by a blind grandmother who symbolizes the older generation giving birth to further situations, but itself remaining fundamentally blind. The grandmother also represents another element, the basic intelligence which is the impetus for stirring up endless clusters of mind/body material, creating such claustrophobia that the crowded situation of the energy sees itself. At this point, the sense of intelligence is undermined and nothing matters but the fundamental deception or loneliness. Simultaneously the overcrowded, clumsy discrimination (thingness, solidified space) is in the way. This is experienced as a subtle irritation combined with subtle absorption. This irritation extends to the grandchild but still remains the grandmother.

This absorption could be called fundamental bewilderment, the "samsaric equivalent of samadhi," an indulgence in something intangible, which is the bewilderment. The solidified space results from trying to confirm this intangible and is the beginning of self-consciousness at that level. You begin to discover that there are possibilities of clinging to intangible qualities as if they were solid. You feel as if there were desolation in the background. You have broken away from something and there's an urge to create habitual patterns. There is a sense of discovery, for you have found some occupation after a whole trip of exploring possibilities, but at the same time you sense the possibility of losing ground forever.

The next nidana presents itself mechanically with the image of a potter's wheel. There is a sense of occupation and responsibility, as though you are a child suddenly condemned to be the director of a big corporation. This second stage is samskara or impulsive accumulation, which enables you to turn the potter's wheel constantly.

But now you are in charge of an individual and quite private game and have a sense of individuality and privacy. At this point, the inkling of a sense of power begins to develop, because you are able to sow a seed or set the wheel in motion. But there is a need of furthering this ambition, which leads to the next nidana—consciousness, or *vijnana*. The symbol for consciousness is a monkey.

The next nidana is a gesture of hope and of a dream coming true. It is *namarupa*, or name and form, symbolized by a person in a boat. When an object has a conceptualized name, it becomes significant. You name the person in terms of your intellectual discoveries and you create the image of the form of the person in accordance with the house (or castle for that matter) which you create. You call it Princess So-and-So or King So-and-So. Name and form are the same. The verbal concept and the visual concept are the same. The names and forms serve as political or philosophical reinforcement. If you have a king or a lord who occupies this particular castle, you would automatically expect that he ought to have an accompanying sense of dignity and that the title should fit the person who occupies this accommodation.

This leads us to the next nidana, *sadayatana*, sensation or sense consciousness, which is represented by a monkey in a six-windowed house. Some kind of a sense of establishment is necessary, purely from the point of view of administration. The six sense organs and the six sense consciousnesses provide a relatively secure home, but still there is the sense of the absence of somebody. Here the whole situation is still tentative and embryonic. In other words, you need to have occupants for the structure, someone quite sophisticated and capable of running the place you've already created. The inquisitive quality of this politician is represented by the monkey, and he is relatively awake as far as his ape qualities can function. There is some paranoia in that you suspect that the castle's occupant is very undignified, because this ape has to function both as guardian and as director. This dual role naturally leads to some sophistication and a sense of diplomacy.

The maintenance of the kingdom leads us to the next

nidana, represented by a married couple. It is *sparsha*, or contact between the masculine and feminine concepts, which complement each other. By trying to capture the fascination and make it into a solid thing, this pair develops a sense of personality and self-respect, which is not based upon domestic affairs alone but also upon foreign relationships.

At this point the next nidana presents itself. This is feeling, *vedana*, which is symbolized by an arrow through the eye. A foreign power introduces itself, but the inquisitive mind pretends to accept this as a delightful surprise, even as a convenience, because it has no choice. There is sharp dramatic feeling, but there is no chance to indulge in a sudden unexpected invitation. You have already magnetized the foreign diplomat (the arrow) and simultaneously you have confirmed your kingdom. It is the first real perception of this and that, which is the world outside. This brings us to the next nidana, *trishna* or *craving*, symbolized by drinking milk and honey.

You are embarrassed because the wholehearted and eager reception of the foreign diplomat was too impulsive, and there is a tendency to tone down. In spite of that tendency, you try your best to relate to him, but at the same time you experience a natural self-indulgence and craving for further contacts which are like the flavor of milk and honey. There is also a tendency to sip and taste and to try to resist swallowing. A possible feeling of repulsion goes through the whole ritual because it is overcrowding, but the impulsive situation takes over and leads us to the next nidana. This is *upadana* or *grasping*, symbolized by gathering fruit.

The subtle manipulation of wishful desire is not enough. There is a tendency to be boyish, to do things as you feel them; you are not concerned with who owns the orchard, but you run out of this stuffy castle and roam around the grounds trying to be outrageous. You pick up fruits and eat them—they are something very definite, lumpy and satisfying. It is very reassuring to hold them, even more so to bite into them without peeling them. At this point, there is an inevitable tendency to feel that someone else could possibly share this experience, or that at least there might be someone to relate to; and this feeling provokes a sense of loneliness and a longing for companionship. This leads us to the next nidana, *bhava* or *becoming*, which is symbolized by copulation.

Bhava celebrates the achievement of relating with another mind/body. It shows new dimensions—the shapes and sculptural qualities of the world are extremely satisfying to feel. It seems that this is the only way of appreciating organic and natural situations. You develop a tremendous awareness of things, including the visual aspect of sense perceptions. At the same time this sensual overindulgence invites valid proof, and you want the evidence of being father or mother to provide a sense of legitimacy. This leads us to the next nidana, *jati* or *birth*, symbolized by a woman in childbirth.

Having given birth to something, a sense of power begins to develop at this point. The simplicity of being creator of the universe is not far away. Becoming goes so far into action that it produces karmic results in this nidana. For example, in a situation of murder, hate gives birth to a corpse. And there are many other possibilities.

But that vitality does not last. The discovery of change becomes irritating and the achievement of this self-indulgence becomes questionable. There is nothing to relate with in terms of continual entertainment; it becomes empty. You have to face the possibility of decay, feebleness, and imminent death. It is inescapable. The exuberance of youth relates to this crescendo of old age, which follows it automatically. Here, extremely cunning intelligence is led to extreme clumsiness in that pure demanding no longer fulfills its function. You see that your game of efficiency is not that efficient after all. But you do not realize that this derelict situation contains another outrageous discovery, which is the next nidana, *jara marana*, or *old age and death*, symbolized by a funeral procession.

Death is the physically overpowering situation of too many things you have to manage. Once upon a time, too many things were exhilarating, but that excitement becomes questionable at this point. The many massive objects and relationships, which you have created, become the inspiration for the charnel ground.

The confused mind finds different styles of occupation. Therefore the six realms of the world can be said to be psychological states, rather than external situations such as a heaven above and a hell below. The realms are known as the whirlpool of illusion—samsara. There is no starting point and no definite order—you can take birth in any realm at any given time. According to the description of the abhidharma, birth into any of the realms is a matter of a sixtieth of a second. And here the concepts of time are also dependent on the involvement in ignorance.

The human realm is said to be the land of karma, because human beings can perceive and work with the karmic force. In this realm, suffering is of the nature of dissatisfaction. The intelligence of human nature itself becomes a source of endless pain. Deliberate self-inflicted struggles lead to the pain of birth, growing up, illness, and death. The constant search for pleasure and its failure pushes the inquisitive intelligence into neurosis. But certain karmic coincidences bring the possibility of realizing the uselessness of struggling, and these coincidences are the particular attribute of the human realm. Therefore the human realm presents the rare opportunity of hearing the Dharma and practicing it.

The solid body and seemingly real situations act as a vessel to preserve the Buddha's teaching, whereas the other realms are so exclusively involved with their own extreme situations that the Dharma cannot be heard, and changes happen only as the karmic force of the hallucinations wears out. The hungry ghost realm is one of an intense state of grasping in the midst of a continual, overwhelming psychological poverty. The definition of hunger in this case is the fear of letting go. There are three types of hungry ghost: the external veil, the internal veil, and the individualist veil. The external veil comes as a result of too much accumulation. You long to become hungrier so you can accumulate even more. The internal veil is having been able to accumulate whatever you want and then the end product becoming something unexpected, usually turning into the reverse, so that the satisfaction turns into dissatisfaction. The individualistic veil is trying any possible way of satisfying your hang-ups, but then a disappointment of a different nature comes in unexpectedly.

Things attack from every direction—wanting and not wanting. This is the state of conflicting emotions.

On the whole, the pain of this realm is not so much that of not finding what you want; rather it is the frustration of wanting itself, which causes excruciating pain.

The stupidity of the animal realm is more that of laziness than that of actual dullness. It contains the refusal to venture onto new ground. There is a tendency to cling to the familiar situation and to fight your way through to still another familiar goal, but this does not contain openness or dance. Another quality of the animal realm is that whenever there is an overpowering force, which might lead you to explore new territory, the immediate reaction is to play dead or to camouflage yourself as though you were not there. The stubbornness of this realm regards individual involvement as very precious, and you are intoxicated with yourself.

The realm of hell is not only the extreme of aggression and its passionate quality, but extends beyond the extreme. This extension backlashes and creates not only a force of energy, but also an all-pervasive environment which is so intense that even the wildness of anger itself finds it unbearable to exist. Therefore there is a tendency to try and escape, and that notion of escape intensifies the imprisonment. Two images have been used to describe this realm. One is intense heat, which creates helplessness, and the realization at the same time that you are radiating this heat yourself. And trying to find a way to turn off the heat becomes too claustrophobic. The other image is intense cold. Any movement toward trying to solve the problem is irritatingly painful; therefore you try to internalize the intense aggression, to freeze it. Although it no longer cuts with a sharp edge in this case, its blunt edge hurts instead.

There is a tendency to commit suicide for the relief of a change of scene, but each moment of change and repetitive birth seems to take millions of years in this realm of hallucinations. There is not a moment to spare for anything other than your own existence in hell. Basically it could be said that because of such paranoia, the pain increases greatly. The process does not allow you a moment for preparation or even to get involved in each instant; there is no pulsation to the pain—it is constant.

The realm of the gods, also known as heaven, is the product of self-indulgence in ideal pleasure. This realm has different degrees; each degree of intensity of pleasure is based on corresponding degrees of maintenance of the pleasure and fear of losing it. The joy of "meditative" absorption saturates your seemingly solid body so that the basic energy is completely undermined. There are occasional flashes of thought, which irritate and bring a tremendous threat to the meditative intoxication.

Basically the reason why the realm of the gods is regarded as an impermanent state is that it is based on ego's game of maintenance in which the meditation is a separate experience from your own being. When the karmic situation of being in heaven wears out, there are suddenly violent thoughts accompanied by suspicion, and the whole blissful state collapses, including the self-conscious concepts of love and the security of being "in love"; another hallucination takes control and you are in another realm.

In the realm of the asuras, or jealous gods, the ambition of gaining a victory or the fear of losing a battle provide a sense of being alive as well as causing irritation. You lose the point of an ultimate goal, but in order to keep the driving force, you have to maintain the ambition. There is a constant desire to be the best, but the sense of losing your game is too real. There is an occasional tendency to punish yourself, so that you learn to strive away from the pain. Whenever you see any pleasurable, appealing situations they seem to be too distant. The desire to bring them close to you is overwhelming, so finally the whole world is built out of golden promises; but it is irritating even to venture to fulfill them.

Sometimes you tend to condemn yourself for not striving for strict discipline and for not achieving the satisfaction of these promises.

This brings us to the center of the wheel of life, which is seen as the path. Having experienced the monotonous and familiar games of the six realms of the world and having heard the Buddhadharma, the truth of pain and the reality of suffering as you have experienced them now bring primordial mind into a state of doubt. At the same time the conclusion arises as a possibility that after all, "things may be just as they are." At that moment the subtler message of the first noble truth begins to click and you are about to sense the meaning of all those useless ventures into the false occupation of ego. The first step is bewilderment, where the teaching is too potent and too true. It seems impossible to be so precise and accurate. It almost feels like a personal insult that there are certain awakened minds and that their teaching can communicate to your basic nature. There is a sense that you have been careless and not able to keep up your secrets.

The first hearing of the teaching is a shock. The sense of inhibition is broken through and therefore personal preservation through ignorance does not apply anymore. Traditionally that ignorance, that deliberate ignoring, is symbolized by the ignoramus pig with its built-in blinkers. It is nondiscriminating perception which relates purely to the sense of survival expressed by consuming whatever comes up, whatever is presented to be consumed.

But that nondiscrimination becomes grasping before the comfortable, snug ignorance finds its place. So this confused venture of passion is depicted in the symbol of the rooster. Passion feels inadequate, so it presents its spiky, sharp points in order to lure like a fishhook, to draw in so that it consumes and attracts attention at the same time. This display by the rooster of its colorful feathers, as well as its beak, can draw in the object of passion; so passion is seen as eliminating the beauty of the phenomenal world. Passion draws in these beauties by a succession of games. Where there is any possible threat to the success of drawing in, it appears that the only possible way of accomplishing the process is to subjugate the object of passion—either by putting out poison to paralyze it or else by overpowering it. This is much the way a snake would proceed, either projecting poison through its fangs or else coiling around that object of desire until it has been completely subdued. Thus the snake is the symbol of aggression. So the whole pattern of aggression and passion is seen as capturing that which is close or else destroying that which is beyond your control. This pattern is at the center of the wheel.

The essence of samsara is found in this turmoil, in this complex situation, as well as in the misunderstandings of bewilderment, passion, and aggression, so the situation also provides the possible means of eliminating these aggravations. But at the same time, unless you relate to these three as path—understanding them, working with them, treading on them—you do not discover the goal. So therefore, as Buddha says, "Suffering should be realized, origin should be overcome and, by that, cessation should be realized because the path should be seen as the truth." Seeing the truth as it is, is the goal as well as the path. For that matter, discovering the truth of samsara is the discovery of nirvana, for truth does not depend on other formulae or alternative answers. The reality of samsara is equally the reality of nirvana. This truth is seen as one truth without relativity.

Reprinted with permission from *The Collected Works of Chögyam Trungpa*, Vol. II, (Boston: Shambhala, 2003), 474–83.

Acknowledgments

SPECIAL THANKS TO my teacher Chögyam Trungpa Rinpoche, without whom I would have continued to cycle through the sand trap of the six realms, oblivious to their true nature.

To my teacher Master Sat Hon for his depth of knowledge and continued support of my journey through the realms and beyond, Seth Freedman, my agent Stephanie Tade, all the folks at Wisdom Publications for their efforts on behalf of this book, Andrew Archer for his wondrously innovative cover art, Ram Dass, Daniel Goleman, Jamie Lee Curtis, Krishna Das, Sharon Salzberg, Pete Holmes, Susan Piver, and Michael Carroll for their kind words, #1 son Ethan Nichtern for our ongoing Dharma dialogue and continuous inspiration, and the ever-lovely Monika Nataraj, who is my companion in our adventure through the realms.

And finally to my mother, Claire Nichtern, and my father, Sol Nichtern, who gave me this precious human birth, and my sister Nicky, who kept the bigger kids from beating me up.

About the Author

DAVID NICHTERN is a senior teacher in the lineage of Chögyam Trungpa Rinpoche—a tradition that combines a contemporary, secular approach to meditation with the ancient practices and philosophies of Tibetan Buddhism. He was one of Trungpa Rinpoche's initial American students and studied closely with him soon after his arrival in the United States in 1970. Over the years he has been co-director of the Shambhala Meditation Center of Los Angeles and the Karmê Chöling meditation center in Vermont, as well as director of expansion for Shambhala Training

International and director of Buddhist practice and study for OM Yoga.

David has been a featured writer and regular contributor to *The Huffington Post* and leads meditation workshops around the world and online. He does a weekly live broadcast on Ustream via his Facebook page and has several online meditation workshops available through creativelive.com. David worked with yoga teacher Cyndi Lee to produce an audio-visual meditation and yoga workshop entitled "OM Yoga and Meditation Workshop," which is widely available.

Nichtern is also a well-known composer, producer, and guitarist, four-time Emmy winner, and a two-time Grammy nominee. He is the founder of Dharma Moon and 5 Points Records. David has recorded and played with Stevie Wonder, Jerry Garcia, Lana Del Rey, Maria Muldaur, Paul Simon, and many others. Among his many credits in records, film, and TV, David was composer and lyricist for the classic song "Midnight at the Oasis," has produced multiple records for Grammy-nominated kirtan performer Krishna Das, and composed the score for Christopher Guest's film *The Big Picture*. Nichtern, Guest, and C. J. Vanston make up The Beyman Bros, and have released an album called *Memories of Summer as a Child*.

Also Available
from Wisdom Publications

THE WHEEL OF LIFE
Buddhist Perspectives on Cause and Effect
His Holiness the Dalai Lama
Translated by Jeffrey Hopkins
Foreword by Richard Gere

"Studded with jewels, pointing out how to bring together the theory of the Buddhist teachings and the practice of ordinary life."—*Shambhala Sun*

MONEY, SEX, WAR, KARMA
Notes for a Buddhist Revolution
David R. Loy

"A flashy title, but a serious and substantial book."
—*Buddhadharma*

A NEW BUDDHIST PATH
Enlightenment, Evolution, and Ethics in the Modern World
David R. Loy

"This gripping, important, and ultimately heartening book by David Loy is a wake-up call for Buddhists and everyone else on how to respond to the current multiple crises."
—Kate Wheeler, author of *When Mountains Walked*

ONE CITY
A Declaration of Interdependence
Ethan Nichtern

"Resonant and refreshing."—*The American Prospect*

About Wisdom Publications

Wisdom Publications is the leading publisher of classic and contemporary Buddhist books and practical works on mindfulness. To learn more about us or to explore our other books, please visit our website at wisdomexperience.org or contact us at the address below.

Wisdom Publications
199 Elm Street
Somerville, MA 02144 USA

We are a 501(c)(3) organization, and donations in support of our mission are tax deductible.

Wisdom Publications is affiliated with the Foundation for the Preservation of the Mahayana Tradition (FPMT).